AA

walking in Wales

First published 2009

Produced by AA Publishing
© AA Media Limited 2009

Published by AA Publishing (a trading name of AA Media Limited, whose registered office is Fanum House, Basing View, Basingstoke, Hampshire RG21 4EA; registered number 06112600)

Visit AA Publishing at theAA.com/bookshop

This product includes mapping data licensed from Ordnance Survey® with the permission of the Controller of Her Majesty's Stationery Office.
© Crown copyright 2009. All rights reserved. Licence number 100021153

ISBN: 978-0-7495-6302-8

A CIP catalogue record for this book is available from the British Library.

Managing Editor: David Popey
Layout and Design: Liz Baldin at Bookwork Creative Associates
Image Retouching and Internal Repro: Sarah Montgomery
Series Design: Liz Baldin at Bookwork Creative Associates for AA Publishing
Cartography provided by the Mapping Services Department of AA Publishing

A04132

Printed by Leo Paper Group in China

PAGES 2–3: Llynnau Mymbyr lake near Capel Curig, with a reflected view to Mount Snowdon
RIGHT: Neuadd Reservoir with Pen y Fan in the background, Brecon Beacons National Park
PAGE 6: A view from Foel Cynwch at Dolgellau, Snowdonia National Park

walking in Wales

Discover castles,

beautiful beaches, lovely lakes

and spectacular peaks

Contents

This superb selection of walks introduces the themes and characters that define the beautiful landscape of Wales.

Introducing Wales

There's something special about crossing the borders into Wales. Maybe it is the way the flat fields of the English shires soar up into the Welsh hills or those veru different-sounding place names on the road signs.

Borderland Wales

Borderland Wales is fertile and verdant, with rolling foothills rising to high, heather moors. Pretty villages set deep into little-known valleys like the Ceirog and the Tanat south of Llangollen just wait to be discovered.

Snowdonia

The Conwy Valley marks the transition to the mountainous heartlands of Wales: Snowdonia. Here the great Carneddau whalebacks decline to the sea, backed by the distinctive craggy Glyderau range and Snowdon itself. All 15 of the 3,000ft (915m) Welsh peaks lie in a compact region between Conwy, Caernarfon and Beddgelert. Villages at the foot of the mountains, like Capel Curig, Betws-y-Coed and Llanberis are dedicated to walkers and climbers. But for those who don't climb, you're never far from the yawning sands of the coast, one of those wonderful narrow-gauge steam railways or one of the great 13th-century castles built by Edward I as part of his 'iron ring' to repress the Welsh warrior princes.

Mid Wales

In absolute contrast to Snowdonia's alpine scenery, the moorland peaks and cwms of the Elenydd region of Mid Wales are simpler in form, with wild and remote upland plateaux opening out to big, big skies. This least-known part of the country contains the source of the mighty Severn

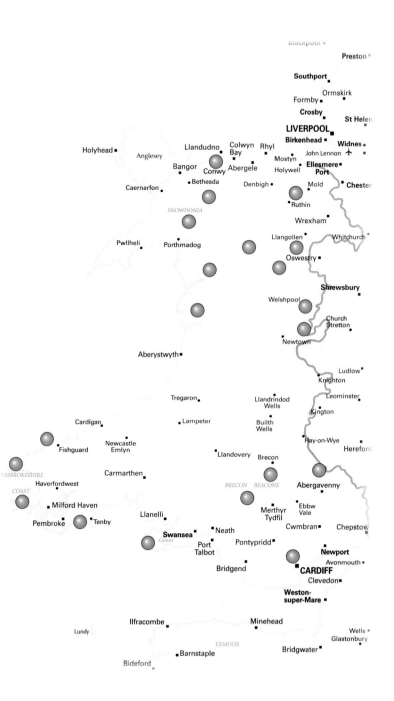

and the Wye: the Welsh 'Lake District', comprising the huge complex of reservoirs of the Vyrnwy, Elan and Clywedog Valleys; and some of the finest stretches of unspoiled coastline, along Cardigan Bay. You can walk here and not see another soul.

South Wales

The great flat-topped sandstone escarpments of the Brecon Beacons mark the entry to South Wales, where rural landscapes descend deep into 'the valleys'. From the Industrial Revolution onwards, the valleys were the engine room of Wales. Coal, iron and steel fuelled an economy that led to massive growth in the ports of Cardiff, Swansea and Newport. The decline of these industries posed challenges but, remembering their maritime roots, towns and cities have been revitalised. Cardiff's vibrant regenerated bay area with its barrage, marinas, Millennium Centre and Senedd Building brings thousands of visitors every week.

Pembrokeshire

Wales meets the Atlantic Ocean at Pembrokeshire, whose spectacular coast is as rugged as anything Cornwall can offer. Unlike the West Country, Pembrokeshire can offer the coast without the crowds, and quaint fishing villages without those huge coach parks. The Welsh coastline is the first part of Britain to receive the influence of the Gulf Stream and at times the effect can seem positively Mediterranean – a scene accentuated in the bizarre village of Portmeirion. The rocky points of the glorious Pembrokeshire coast stretch out into the blue waters of the Irish Sea, haunted by seabirds, and its cliff-hemmed sandy bays are perfect for water-sports. The gorse-studded peninsula of the Gower, with its quiet beaches, coves and charming fishing villages, has long been the playground of the industrial cities of South Wales.

Walking Year-Round

Wales lies on the western side of Britain, and often receives more than its fair share from laden rain clouds sweeping in from the North Atlantic. Good waterproofs will therefore make any time walking

using this book

Information Panels
An information panel for each walk shows its relative difficulty, the distance and total amount of ascent. An indication of the gradients you will encounter is shown by the rating ▲▲▲▲ (no steep slopes) to ▲▲▲▲ (several very steep slopes). The minimum time suggested for the walk is for reasonably fit walkers and doesn't allow for stops.

Suggested Maps
Each walk has a suggested Ordnance Survey Explorer map.

Start Points
The start of each walk is given as a six-figure grid reference prefixed by two letters indicating which 100-km square of the National Grid it refers to. You'll find more information on grid references on most Ordnance Survey maps.

Dogs
We have tried to give dog owners useful advice about the dog friendliness of each walk. Please respect other countryside users. Keep your dog under control, especially around livestock, and obey local bylaws and other dog-related notices.

Car Parking
Many of the car parks suggested are public, but occasionally you may find you have to park on the roadside or in a lay-by. Please be considerate when you leave your car, ensuring that access roads or gates are not blocked and that other vehicles can pass safely.

Maps
Each walk in this book is accompanied by a map based on Ordnance Survey information. The scale of these maps varies from walk to walk.

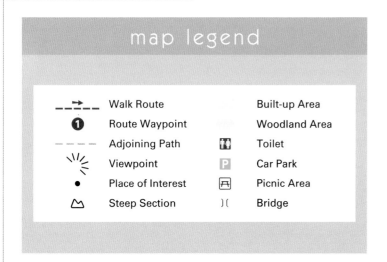

map legend

‑‑‑→‑‑	Walk Route		Built-up Area
❶	Route Waypoint		Woodland Area
‑ ‑ ‑	Adjoining Path	🚻	Toilet
☀	Viewpoint	P	Car Park
•	Place of Interest	🪑	Picnic Area
⌂	Steep Section	)(	Bridge

here a little more comfortable. The terrain tends to be rougher than its equivalents in England – the coastal paths are steeper, the mountains tend to be higher and, in the north at least, considerably rockier. Fewer people walk in the valleys, and you will find the paths here muddier and generally less well trodden. Pay particular attention to the weather forecasts before you set out. All-enveloping hill fog can descend at almost any time, making navigation demanding even for experienced hillwalkers. Winter conditions in the mountains can turn even the most innocuous outing into a dangerous adventure if you are not suitably equipped. You should also carry plenty of warm clothing, waterproof trousers, a survival bag, torch, spare food and water. On coastal routes make sure you check the tides and weather forecast before setting out. Happily there is often a strip of blue sky, which lines the coast, so it's not unknown to be sunbathing on the sands just a few hours after battling the wind and rain in the hills.

RIGHT: St David's Head, Pembrokeshire National Park

*Conwy's magnificent castle lies at the foot of
the Carneddau, but up there in the foothills
there's a fort, an outpost of the Celtic era.*

Conwy: Castle High and Castle Low

*ABOVE: The 13th-century Conwy Castle's eight
grey-stone towers stand overlooking Conwy
LEFT: Telford's Suspension Bridge stretches
dramatically away from Conwy Castle*

Conwy is special. Approaching from Llandudno Junction, three fine bridges (including Thomas Telford's magnificent suspension bridge of 1822) cross the estuary beneath the mighty castle, allowing the road and the railway into this medieval World Heritage Site. The fortress dates back to 1287, when the powerful English King Edward I built it as part of his 'iron ring' to repress the rebellious troops of Llewelyn the Great, who had given him a great deal of trouble in his conquest of Wales.

Rooftop Views

Great town walls with gates and towers still encircle old Conwy. You should walk these walls, for they offer a fine rooftop view of the castle, the Conwy Estuary and the rocky knolls of Deganwy, before you arrive at the quayside where you can watch the fishermen sorting their nets and the seagulls watching out for any scraps. The walk description begins at the quayside, not the car park, as you will probably want to take a good look around this medieval town. The route starts on a shoreline path under the boughs of Bodlondeb Wood.

The Ancient Settlements of Conwy Mountain

Not long after passing through Conwy's suburbs you're walking the hillside, on a path threading through gorse and small wind-twisted hawthorns. If you liked the views from the castle walls, you'll love the view from the Conwy Mountain ridge. Looking back you can see the castle, towering over the town's roof tops; but now added to the scene are the Carneddau, the limestone isthmus of the Great Orme and, across the great sands of Lafan, Anglesey.

There is quite a network of paths criss-crossing the ridge and usually the best course is the highest: you'll need to be on the crest path to see the remains of Castell Caer. This 10-acre (4ha) fort has been linked to both Roman and Iron Age settlers – it certainly has formidable defences, with clearly visible artificial ramparts that overlook spectacular sea cliffs on one side, and a wide view of the land to the south. Beyond the fort, the path misses out the peaks of Penmaen-bach and Alltwen, which is just as well, for the former has been heavily quarried for its roadstone – you probably drove over some of it on your way up the motorway. Instead you should descend to the Sychnant Pass, a splendid, twisting gorge that separates Conwy Mountain from the higher Carneddau peaks.

It's all downhill from here, but the scenery becomes more varied and still maintains interest. As you descend you can see the tidal River Conwy, twisting amongst chequered green fields. Little hills present themselves to you, on your way back north. One last hill has pleasant woods with primroses and bluebells, and it gives you another fine view of Conwy Castle to add to your collection before returning to base.

RIGHT: The heather on Mynydd y Dref (Conwy Mountain)
slopes gently towards Penmaenbach

walk directions

3 Several tracks converge in the high fields of Pen-Pyra. Here, follow signposts for the North Wales Path along the track heading to the south-west over the left shoulder of Alltwen and down to the metalled road traversing the Sychnant Pass.

1 From Conwy Quay head north-west along the waterfront, past the Smallest House and under the town walls. Fork right along a tarmac waterside footpath that rounds Bodlondeb Wood. Turn left along the road, past the school and on to the A547. Cross the road, then the railway line by a footbridge. The track beyond skirts a wood to reach a lane, where you turn right.

4 Follow the footpath from the other side of the road, skirting the woods on your left. Over a stile carry on past Gwern Engen to meet a track. Go right and then bear left, dropping above the Lodge to reach a lane. Turn right along the lane, then turn left, when you reach the next junction, into Groesffordd village. Cross the road, then take the road ahead that swings to the right past a telephone box, then left (south east) towards Plas Iolyn.

2 At a fork bear right past a house to a waymarked stile, from which a footpath rakes up wooded hillsides up on to Conwy Mountain. Follow the undulating crest of Conwy Mountain and continue past Castell Caer.

5 Turn left at the end but then leave opposite a white house on a path climbing to a cottage. Cross a track and continue upfield to the B5106.

walk information

➤ **DISTANCE**	6.75 miles (10.9km)
➤ **MINIMUM TIME**	4hrs
➤ **ASCENT/GRADIENT**	1,493ft (455m) ▲▲▲
➤ **LEVEL OF DIFFICULTY**	👤👤👤
➤ **PATHS**	Good paths and easy-to-follow moorland tracks, 5 stiles
➤ **LANDSCAPE**	Town, coastline high ridge, farmland and copsee
➤ **SUGGESTED MAPS**	OS Explorer OL17 Snowdon
➤ **START/FINISH**	Grid reference: SH 783775
➤ **DOG FRIENDLINESS**	OK on high ridges, but keep on lead elsewhere
➤ **PARKING**	Large car park on Llanrwst Road behind Conwy Castle
➤ **PUBLIC TOILETS**	At car park

Go left to Conwy Touring Park. Follow the drive to a hairpin, from which a waymarked path climbs through trees, recrossing the drive. Finally emerging through a kissing gate, continue up the field edge. Swing left along an undulating ridge above successive pastures, finally meeting a lane.

6 Turn left, shortly leaving right along a track past a communications mast to Bryn-locyn. Continue at the edge of fields beyond to a stile by Coed Benarth, from which a path drops beside the wood.

7 Go over a ladder stile on your left-hand side and descend a field to a roadside gate at the bottom. Turn right on to the B5106 to return to the quayside, or turn left to get back to the main car park.

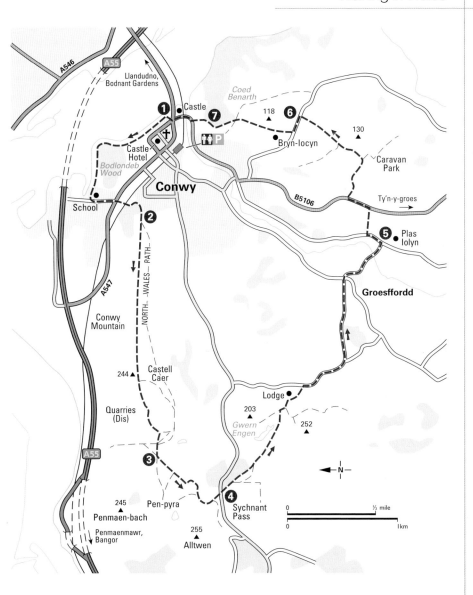

LEFT: Conwy Castle's eight towers and high curtain wall dominate the town of Conwy

Walk to the highest of the Clwydian Hills and see a beautiful wooded limestone valley on the way.

Moel Famau: the Mother Mountain

If you're driving into Wales from the north-west, the chances are that the first hills you'll see are the Clwydians, dark rolling ridges that rise up from the sea at Prestatyn and decline 20 miles (32km) or so south in the fields of the Alun Valley. Although the hills are empty these days, at one time they were highly populated. Climb to the tops and you'll see Iron and Bronze Age forts scattered about the hilltops, some of them among the best preserved in Wales.

ABOVE: *Jubilee Tower stands at the top of Moel Famau*
RIGHT: *Sunset adds a touch of gold to the Vale of Clwyd*

At Loggerheads

One of the best places to start a walk in the Clwydians is Loggerheads. The path from the information centre follows the shallow, swift-flowing River Alun through a narrow limestone valley filled with wych elm and oak. In July, you'll see limestone flora, including field scabious, wild thyme, rock rose and bloody cranesbill, while above there are spotted woodpeckers, tawny owls and nuthatches.

On the Top

The climb out of the valley includes a short traverse of farmland before clambering through heather fields to Moel Famau, which means 'mother mountain' and at 1,818ft (554m) is the highest of the range. The monument on the summit was built in 1810 to celebrate the jubilee of King George III after 50 years on the throne. Its square tower and spire were wrecked by a violent gale some 50 years later, and the place lay in ruins until 1970 when it was tidied up.

Below and to the west there's the much older site of Moel y Gaer, one of those fascinating hill-forts with concentric earthwork rings sculpted into a grassy knoll.

Casting your eyes beyond the rings and across the green fields and chequered hedgerows of the Vale of Clwyd, it's interesting to pick out the familiar skyline summits of Snowdonia. Tryfan's jagged crest is easy to spot, but somehow you cannot quite see Snowdon and that's because Moel Siabod, prima donna that it feels it is, has elbowed its way to the front, to hide the real star of the show, Snowdon, and confuse the issue. Fortunately there are topographs to help you out.

The ridge walking from the summit is delightful. A wide path takes you down to the forest, where it continues down a grassy ride. While the spruce trees are not an attractive habitat for a wide range of species you might easily spot a song thrush, colourful chaffinches or coal tits; or maybe, just maybe, a sparrowhawk. Country lanes and farm pastures take you down to the banks of the River Alun which guides you back to Loggerheads and the car park.

walk directions

1 Go past the front of the Loggerheads Country Park Information Centre, café and other buildings, cross the bridge over the Alun and turn left along the surfaced path through the valley. Keep to the main, near-level path, marked the Leete Path.

2 Pass the A.L.Y.N. Kennels, cross a lane, then look out for a small, often slippery path on the left (signed Moel Famau). This leads to a footbridge. Across this the path heads west, then staggers to the right across a farm lane and climbs past a farmhouse. Enclosed by thickets, it climbs to the right of another house to reach a T-junction of country lanes. Go straight ahead and follow the lane uphill, then turn right to follow the track that passes Ffrith farm before swinging left to climb round the pastured slopes of Ffrith Mountain. Take the left fork in the tracks (at grid ref 177637).

3 The route skirts a spruce plantation and climbs to a crossroads of tracks, marked by a tall waymarker post. Turn left here on a wide path over undulating heather slopes towards the tower on the top of Moel Famau.

4 From the summit, head south-east and go through a gate at the end of the wall to follow a wide track, marked with red-tipped waymarker posts, south-east along the forest's edge. The track continues its descent through the trees to meet the roadside car park/picnic area 0.75 mile (1.2km) east of Bwlch Penbarra's summit (See Information Panel on using shuttle bus).

5 Turn left along the road, before turning right when you get to the first junction. The quiet lane leads to the busy A494. Cross the main road with care and continue along the hedge-lined lane staggered to the right.

6 A waymarked path on the left heads north-east across fields towards the banks of the Alun. Don't cross the river at the bridge, but head north, through the gateway and across more fields, passing a stone-built house below on the right. Turn right on the A494. It's just 0.5 mile (800m) from here to the Loggerheads Country Park entrance, and there are verges and paths to walk on.

walk information

➤ **DISTANCE**	8 miles (12.9km)
➤ **MINIMUM TIME**	4hrs 30min
➤ **ASCENT/GRADIENT**	1,608ft (490m) ▲▲▲
➤ **LEVEL OF DIFFICULTY**	ΛΛΛ
➤ **PATHS**	Well-defined paths and forestry tracks, 8 stiles
➤ **LANDSCAPE**	Heather moor, forest and farmland
➤ **SUGGESTED MAPS**	OS Explorer 265 Clwydian Range
➤ **START/FINISH**	Grid reference: SJ 198625
➤ **DOG FRIENDLINESS**	Dogs could run free in forest and on heather ridges
➤ **PARKING**	Pay car park by Loggerheads Country Park Visitor Centre
➤ **PUBLIC TOILETS**	At Visitor Centre
➤ **NOTE**	Route can be shortened by taking regular Moel Famau shuttle bus, which runs on Sundays (July to September) and bank holidays, from forestry car park to Loggerheads

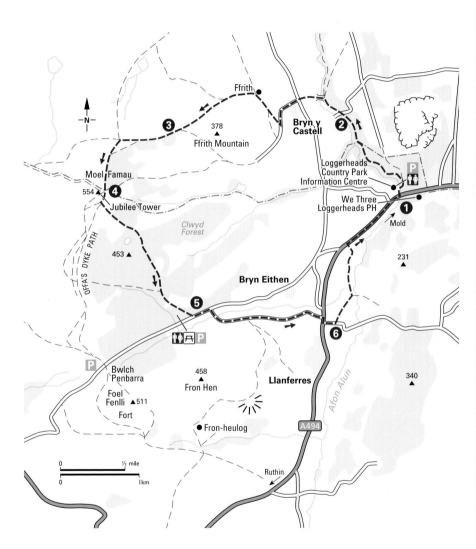

Discovering the valley where

rocks and the mountains are

still all important.

An Alpine Journey Above the Llugwy

'I descended a great steep into Glan Llugwy, a bottom watered by the Llugwy, fertile in grass and varied by small groves of young oaks… The small church of Capel Curig, and a few scattered houses give life to this dreary tract. Yr Wyddfa and all his sons, Crib Goch, Crib y Ddysgl, Lliwedd, Yr Aran and many others here burst at once into full view and make this the finest approach to our boasted Alps'

Thomas Pennant, *A Tour in Wales*, 1778

The description holds true today, for nowhere has one village been so strung out – Capel Curig's sparse cottages and inns stretch 6 miles (9.7km) between Pont-Cyfyng, beneath Moel Siabod, to the Pen y Gwryd, beneath Glyder Fawr.

ABOVE: *A ruined farmhouse near Capel Curig*
LEFT: *The reflective waters of Llynnau Mymbyr lake near Capel Curig*

A New Breed of Visitor

The link still lies in those alps. The well-spaced inns were positioned there, at first to serve the quarrymen from the barracks of Siabod and the miners from the copper mines of Snowdon, then, when the mines and quarries shut down, that new breed of visitor, the walker and the climber. These inns were a convenient meeting place. Geoffrey Winthrop Young was one of the first, but many followed, pioneering new routes on the crags. Quickly Capel Curig became the Zermatt of Wales, and Snowdon, the Matterhorn. In the 1950s the Pen y Gwryd Inn, run by enthusiast Chris Biggs, became a centre for planning Alpine and Himalayan expeditions. Here Lord Hunt and his team, who in 1953 were the first to climb Everest, met to make the final preparations before departing for Nepal. The Climbers' Bar has a wood ceiling that has been autographed by many world famous climbers, including the summit pair, Sir Edmund Hillary and Tenzing Norgay.

This walk will round the valley, taking in views of the wide sweep of mountains that surround Capel Curig and the Llugwy Valley.

To the Woods

You continue through those oak woods seen by Pennant, now wonderfully matured, before descending back down to the boisterous river. In front of the Ty'n y Coed Inn they have one of the old London to Holyhead stagecoaches on display. After crossing the river at Pont-Cyfyng you follow its delightful banks for a short while, then go over crag, across pasture and through the woods. You come out by a footbridge on the shores of Llynnau Mymbyr, and again you see Snowdon, maybe still perfectly reflected in glass-like waters. On the other side of the bridge at the Plas y Brenin National Mountain Centre, they're training the next generation of mountaineers.

RIGHT: Capel Curig seen across the blue waters of Llynnau Mymbyr lake

ABOVE: Capel Curig (foreground) is located in the heart of Snowdonia; Mount Snowdon looms in the distance

walk directions

1 The path begins at a ladder stile by the war memorial on the A5 and climbs towards Y Pincin, a large craggy outcrop cloaked in wood and bracken. Go over another stile and keep to the left of the outcrop. Those who want to go to the top should do so from the north-east, where the gradients are easier. It's fun, but take care! You'll need to retrace your steps to the main route.

2 Continue east through woods and across marshy ground, keeping well to the right of the great crags of Clogwyn-mawr. On reaching a couple of ladder stiles, ignore the footpath, right, back down to the road, but maintain your direction across the hillside.

3 Just beyond a footbridge over Nant y Geuallt, leave the main footpath and follow a less well-defined one, with marker posts, across marshy ground. This path veers south-east to cross another stream before coming to a track.

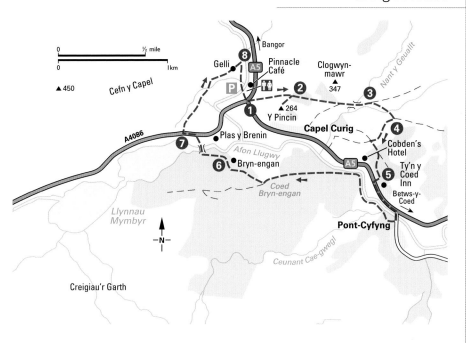

walk information

➤ **DISTANCE**	4 miles (6.4km)
➤ **MINIMUM TIME**	2hrs
➤ **ASCENT/GRADIENT**	295ft (90m) ▲▲▲
➤ **LEVEL OF DIFFICULTY**	🚶🚶🚶 (doesn't include pinnacle scramble)
➤ **PATHS**	Generally clear and surfaced but can be wet in places, 9 stiles
➤ **LANDSCAPE**	Woodland, wetland and high pasture
➤ **SUGGESTED MAPS**	OS Explorer OL17 Snowdon
➤ **START/FINISH**	Grid reference: SJ 720582
➤ **DOG FRIENDLINESS**	Dogs should be on lead
➤ **PARKING**	Behind Joe Brown's shop at Capel Curig
➤ **PUBLIC TOILETS**	By Joe Brown's shop

4 Turn right along the track, go over a ladder stile, then at a four-way meeting of paths head left. Follow the path descending into some woods. Take the right-hand fork descending to the road near Ty'n y Coed Inn.

5 Turn left down the road, then right, along the lane over Pont-Cyfyng. Go right again beyond the bridge to follow a footpath that traces the Llugwy to another bridge opposite Cobdens Hotel. Don't cross this time, but scramble left over some rocks before continuing through the woods of Coed Bryn-engan, where the path soon becomes a wide track.

6 After passing the cottage of Bryn-engan, the track comes to the bridge at the head of the Mymbyr lakes. Turn right across it, then go left along the road for a short way.

7 Cross the road to the next ladder stile and take a track straight ahead, soon swinging right to hug the foot of the southern Glyder slopes.

8 When you get beyond Gelli farm turn right to follow the cart track back to the car park.

A walk up to the old copper mines of Mynydd Sygn and through the spectacular Pass of Aberglaslyn.

There's Copper in Them There Hills

This route heads for the rugged hills forming one side of the great Aberglaslyn gorge that has graced many a postcard and book jacket. At the back of the car park you pass under a railway bridge that belonged to the Welsh Highland Railway and pass the site of an old crushing plant. Here, copper ore from the mountain would have been prepared for shipment, using the railway.

ABOVE: *The fast flowing Afon Glaslyn, cuts out of the Snowdonia mountains*
RIGHT: *The view from the Afon Glaslyn river towards Aberglaslyn Gorge*

Cwm Bychan

Beyond the plant, the path follows a playful stream and climbs steadily through the lonely Cwm Bychan. Here, beneath splintered, craggy mountains patched with heather and bracken, you come across a line of rusting gantries. They're part of an old aerial ropeway, built to carry ore down to the crushing mill. Mining had taken place hereabouts since Roman times, but after World War One the extraction became uneconomical. In 1922 the mines closed.

Continuing to the col above, the route comes to a huge area of mining spoil and a meeting of routes. Ours turns south, and soon we're following a rugged rocky path zig-zagging down to a grassy basin below before continuing along a craggy ridge. Here the ground drops away steeply into the valley of the Afon Glaslyn. If it's early summer the scene will be emblazoned by the vivid pink blooms of rhododendrons, which smother the hillside. Hundreds of feet below lie the roof tops of Beddgelert and what lies in-between is a glorious little path twisting through those rhododendrons and the rocks into the village. If you get that feeling of déjà vu the hillsides around here were used for the setting of the Chinese village in *The Inn of the Sixth Happiness* (1958), starring Ingrid Bergman.

Beddgelert is a pretty village with a fine two-arched bridge spanning the Glaslyn and a handful of busy craft shops and cafés, which throng with visitors in the summer. Around here they're all too fond of telling you the story of Prince Llewelyn's brave dog, Gelert, and pointing to the grave which gave the village its name. Don't be misled; a past landlord of the Royal Goat devised the plausible story to boost his trade. We're going to head for the great gorge of Aberglaslyn!

The Gorge

The way back to Aberglaslyn used to be by way of the old Welsh Highland Railway trackbed, but since this has been reopened the only route is now a rough track by the raging river. The hard bit with handholds comes early on. If you can manage that you can enjoy the excitement of a walk through the gorge and through the attractive woodland that shades its banks. If you want to see that postcard view though, you'll have to make a short detour to the roadside at Pont Aberglaslyn. It's stunning if you haven't seen it before.

walk information

➤ **DISTANCE**	4 miles (6.4km)
➤ **MINIMUM TIME**	2hrs 30min
➤ **ASCENT/GRADIENT**	1,181ft (360m) ▲▲▲
➤ **LEVEL OF DIFFICULTY**	🎄🎄🎄🎄
➤ **PATHS**	Well-maintained paths and tracks (see note below), 2 stiles
➤ **LANDSCAPE**	Rocky hills and river gorge
➤ **SUGGESTED MAPS**	OS Explorer OL17 Snowdon
➤ **START/FINISH**	Grid reference: SH 597462
➤ **DOG FRIENDLINESS**	Dogs should be on lead at all times
➤ **PARKING**	National Trust pay car park, Aberglaslyn
➤ **PUBLIC TOILETS**	At car park
➤ **NOTE**	Short section of riverside path in Aberglaslyn gorge is difficult and requires use of handholds

walk directions

1 The path starts to the left of the toilet block and goes under the old railway bridge, before climbing through Cwm Bychan. After a steady climb the path reaches the iron pylons of the aerial cableway.

2 Beyond the pylons, keep straight on, ignoring paths forking left. A grassy corridor leads to a col, where there's a stile in a fence that is not shown on current maps. Bear left beyond the stile and head for a three-way footpath signpost by the rocks of Grib Ddu.

3 Follow the path on the left signed 'To Beddgelert and Sygun' and go over another ladder stile. Turn left, then follow the path down round a rocky knoll and then down the hillside to a signpost. Just beyond the sign is the cairn at Bwlch-y-Sygyn and over to the left is a shallow, peaty pool in a green hollow.

4 The path now heads south-west along the mountain's north-western ridge, overlooking Beddgelert. Ignore any lesser paths along the way.

5 Watch out for a large cairn, highlighting the turn-off right for Beddgelert. The clear stony path weaves through rhododendron and rock, goes through a kissing gate in a wall half-way down, then descends further to the edge of Beddgelert, where a little lane passing the cottage of Penlan leads to the Afon Glaslyn.

6 Turn left to follow the river for a short way. Don't cross the footbridge over the river but turn left to follow the Glaslyn's east bank. Cross the restored railway line and then continue between it and the river.

7 Below the first tunnel, the path is pushed right to the water's edge. Handholds screwed into the rocks assist passage on a difficult but short section. The path continues through riverside woodland and over boulders until it comes to Pont Aberglaslyn.

8 Here, turn left up some steps and follow a dirt path through the woods. Just before the railway, follow a signed path down and right to the car park.

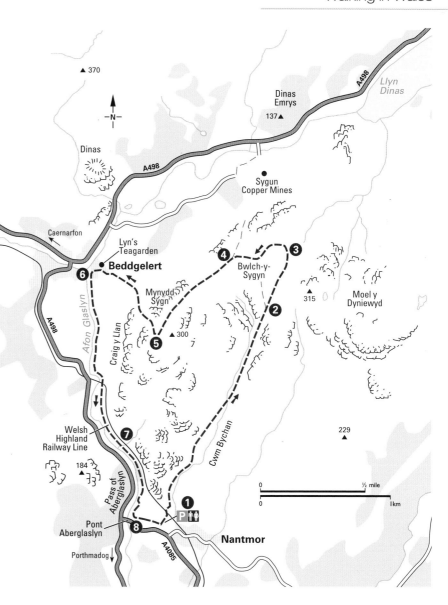

Climbing above Bala to get the best view of Wales' largest natural lake.

A View of Bala's Lake – Llyn Tegid

'It was a beautiful evening…the wind was blowing from the south, and tiny waves were beating against the shore, which consisted of small brown pebbles. The lake has certainly not its name, which signifies Lake of Beauty, for nothing'
George Borrow, Wild Wales, 1862

Borrow had been staying at the White Lion in Bala and had been impressed with the place and its people. Bala is an austere town, close to the banks of two great rivers, the Tryweryn and the Dee, and the shore of Wales' largest natural lake, Llyn Tegid.

ABOVE: Bala Lake miniature railway
LEFT: Sailors enjoy all that George Borrow's 'Lake of Beauty' has to offer

Religion and Wool

The town's many chapels give a hint to its religious roots. You'll see the statue of Dr Lewis Edwards, founder of the Methodist College, and, opposite the White Lion, one of the Revd Thomas Charles, a founder of the British and Foreign Bible Society. Bala's employment was based around the woollen industry, and the town was noted for its stockings. Thomas Pennant came here in 1786 and painted a fascinating picture of life in the town: 'Round the place, women and children are in full employ, knitting along the roads; and mixed with them Herculean figures appear, assisting their omphales in this effeminate employ.'

Recreational Activities

Llyn Tegid is every bit as beautiful as Borrow suggests and it's popular for watersports. When the south-westerlies blow, Bala has waves like an angry ocean. It's favoured by anglers too. Pike, perch, trout, salmon and roach are plentiful, but the fish Llyn Tegid is famous for is the Gwyniad, which is not unlike a freshwater herring. It is said these fish were trapped here after the last ice age. You come to the old Norman motte-and-bailey castle of Tomen y Mur soon after turning your back on the lake. Some say that the mound goes back to Roman times, but it is known that the castle was captured from the Normans by Llewelyn ap Iowerth in 1202. One of those Welsh steam railways has its terminus right next to the old castle site and it's fascinating to see the old steam engines puffing along the lakeside. However, we are in search of higher things, so climb through woods and upland fields until you get your view. From up high you can see Tegid's blue waters, seemingly perfect and still from this distance, and stretching 4.5 miles (7.2km) along its rift valley towards Dolgellau. White farmhouses are dotted on pleasant pastured hills. The Dee, so wide down river from Bala, has anonymous beginnings in the peat bogs beneath Dduallt, whose dark crags rise high on the north-west horizon. It's time to descend, through more oak woods, and further, beneath western hemlock and larch, finally to reach the lakeshores and the welcome comforts of the town.

RIGHT: The Bala Lake Railway uses a 2ft (610mm) narrow gauge steam train

walk directions

1 Go to the north corner of the car park in Bala to access the riverside path. Turn right to follow a raised embankment along the west bank of the Tryweryn. After a dog-leg to the right, passing through two kissing gates, the footpath continues, first by the banks of the Tryweryn, then by the north banks of the Dee.

2 On reaching the road, cross the bridge over the River Dee, then a smaller, older bridge. Go through a kissing gate to cross a small field to Bala Station on Bala Lake Railway. A footbridge allows you to cross the track before traversing two small fields.

3 Turn right along a cart track, and continue to pass behind the Bala Lake Hotel. A waymarker points the direction up a grassy bank on the left, and the path continues to a stile and then follows a fence on the right.

4 Descend slightly to cross a stream beside a small cottage, go up again then along a level fence to a stile. Bear left up through some bracken and wind up steeply at first, then continue more easily to a tarmac lane.

5 Turn left along the lane to a cattle grid from where you continue on a stony track, passing through felled plantations.

6 Just before the isolated house of Cefn-ddwygraig, turn left off the track to a ladder stile. Follow a grooved grass track across gorse-covered slopes. Keep left at a fork and then drop down to a stile. The well-waymarked path continues north, with Bala town ahead.

7 Go over a partially hidden step stile into the commercial forestry plantations of Coed Pen-y-bont. A narrow footpath descends to the bottom edge of the woods (ignore the forestry track you meet on the way down).

8 At the bottom of the woods turn right along a track that reaches the road by the Pen-y-Bont Campsite. Turn left along the road, cross the Dee again, bear left and then follow the lakeside footpath past the information centre. When you reach the main road, turn right to explore the fascinating town centre.

walk information

➤ **DISTANCE**	5 miles (8km)
➤ **MINIMUM TIME**	3hrs
➤ **ASCENT/GRADIENT**	656ft (200m) ▲▲▲
➤ **LEVEL OF DIFFICULTY**	🚶🚶🚶
➤ **PATHS**	Woodland and field paths, 7 stiles
➤ **LANDSCAPE**	Woods and upland pasture
➤ **SUGGESTED MAPS**	OS Explorer OL23 Cadair Idris & Llyn Tegid, or OS Explorer OL18 Harlech, Porthmadog and Bala
➤ **START/FINISH**	Grid reference: SH 929361
➤ **DOG FRIENDLINESS**	Dogs should be on lead at all times
➤ **PARKING**	Car park at entrance to Bala town from east
➤ **PUBLIC TOILETS**	At car park

LEFT: Spectators watch the water-sports on the scenic Llyn Tegid

37

*Discover an earthly heaven in one
of ancient Clwyd's truly green and
pleasant valleys.*

In the Beautiful Ceiriog Valley

*ABOVE: One of the pretty village gardens in
Llanarmon Dyffryn Ceiriog
LEFT: Llanarmon Dyffryn Ceiriog's name is
derived from the 5th-century missionary,
St Garmon*

David Lloyd George, the last Liberal Party Prime Minister of Britain, described the Ceiriog Valley as 'a piece of heaven that has fallen to earth'. For 18 miles (29km), from its source on the slopes of Mount Fferna in the Berwyns to its meeting with the Dee, the beautiful Afon Ceiriog meanders through oak woods, rocky hillsides and fertile cattle pastures. Yet in 1923 city planners wanted to turn this little piece of heaven into a huge reservoir. If these planners had won the day, the locals living within an area of 13,600 acres (5,508ha) would have been evicted from their homes. Fortunately Parliament denied their whims.

St Garmon

While Glyn Ceiriog is the largest village, Llanarmon Dyffryn Ceiriog is the most beautiful. Lying by the confluence of the Ceiriog and a tributary, the Gwrachen, it was a natural fording place for drovers bound for the markets of England. You'll be using some of their old roads on this walk. The village and its church take their name from the 5th-century missionary, St Garmon. The present church is early Victorian and, unusually, has two pulpits. A mound in the churchyard, known as Tomen Garmon, is believed to be a Bronze Age burial mound and the place where the missionary preached.

A Pastoral Idyll

The walk begins behind the church, and follows pretty pastures above the Ceiriog and woods full of bluebells before coming to the old Mill (Y Felin) at Tregeiriog. In the 19th century, author George Borrow revelled in the pastoral nature of this landscape. He spent hours standing on the bridge, watching pigs foraging by the river bank while the old Mill's waterwheel slowly turned; a scene he said that 'was well-suited to the brushes of two or three of the old Dutch painters'.

From the old Mill the route climbs on one of those drovers' roads on to the small hills overlooking the valley. You can see many a mile of rolling green hills as a winding green track climbs towards some crags on the horizon. Here you enter a wilder world of rushy moorland with views down the valleys of Nant y Glôg and the Gwrachen. After tramping through the bracken of the high hillside you join another green road which accompanies the Gwrachen. By now you may be following the footsteps of Owain Glyndwr, 15th-century Prince of Wales, who would have passed through Llanarmon when travelling between his residences at Sycharth and Glyndyfrdwy in the Dee Valley.

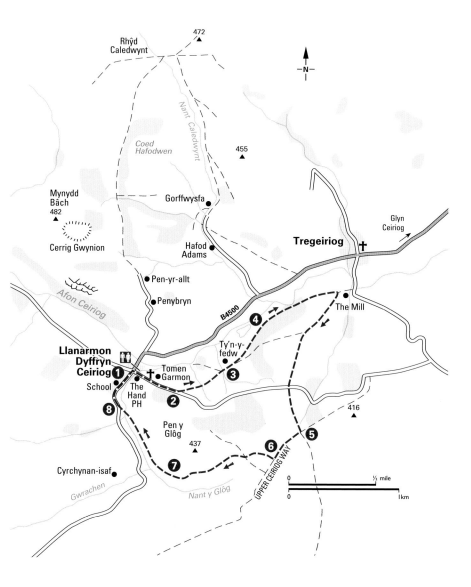

RIGHT: A fence covered in colourful hanging baskets in Llanarmon Dyffryn Ceiriog

walk directions

1 From The Hand, take the eastbound lane past the church and uphill with a conifer plantation on the right and the pastures of the Ceiriog below left.

2 At the far end of the plantation leave the road for a farm track on the left. This ends at a barn. Keep to the right of the barn and aim for a gate beyond it. Through the gate maintain your direction, over the shoulder of a grassy knoll, then aim for a stile in a fence ahead. Beyond this, cross another field down to a gate, through which mount a stile on the right.

3 Bear left, crossing two streamlets to join a track past Ty'n-y-fedw farm. Don't go through the gate, but follow a grass path right beside the fence, shortly entering a wood

4 Keep ahead to the far end of the woods. Emerging into a field, a grass trod curves round to a gate at the top corner. Turn right along a rising farm track, ignoring junctions to reach a lane. Next cross to the ongoing track opposite, which climbs on through the high pastures.

5 At a crossroads, turn right along a green track – part of the Upper Ceiriog Way. This heads south-west towards the green hill known as Cefn-Hîr-fynydd.

6 After about 300yds (274m) leave this track through a gate on the right. If you head west by the right edge of the rushy area and towards Pen y Glôg's sparse crags, it will be easy to find the small stile in the next fence, then the wooden gate on the left soon afterwards. Through the gate head downhill with a faint sheep path past a low clump of rocks on the left, and aiming for the distant farm of Cyrchynan-isaf.

7 Lower down, a developing grassy track runs on through the valley of Nant y Glôg contouring the lower slopes of Pen y Glôg, and eventually reaching a gate.

8 After swinging right with the lively stream the track terminates by a lane to the south of Llanarmon Dyffryn Ceiriog. Follow the lane past several attractive cottages and the village school to arrive by the Hand hotel in the village square.

walk information

➤ DISTANCE	3.75 miles (6km)
➤ MINIMUM TIME	2hrs 30min
➤ ASCENT/GRADIENT	853ft (260m)
➤ LEVEL OF DIFFICULTY	
➤ PATHS	Sketchy paths and farm tracks, 4 stiles
➤ LANDSCAPE	Pastoral hillscapes and river scenery
➤ SUGGESTED MAPS	OS Explorer 255 Llangollen & Berwyn
➤ START/FINISH	Grid reference: SJ 157328
➤ DOG FRIENDLINESS	Whole walk through sheep country, keep dogs on lead
➤ PARKING	Roadside parking in village
➤ PUBLIC TOILETS	At village hall

*A demanding, but short walk
brings magnificent views and
a visit to spectacular falls.*

Cadair Berwyn and Pistyll Rhaeadr

*ABOVE: Pistyll Rhaeadr, Wales'
tallest waterfall tumbles 240ft (73m) from
the Berwyn Mountains
LEFT: Purple foxgloves on the side of a wooded
valley near Pistyll Rhaeadr*

'What shall I liken it to? I scarcely know, unless to an immense skein of silk agitated and disturbed by tempestuous blasts, or to the long tail of a grey courser at furious speed.'

This is how author, George Borrow saw the falls of Pistyll Rhaeadr in his travels in *Wild Wales* (1862). The mountain valley, fringed by crag and dappled with heather and bracken, leads to Llyn Lluncaws. Here's a dramatic scene – a wild Welsh cwm in which the lake lies dark and sombre among frazzled heather that can't quite take hold and tussocky moor grass that fills in the extra spaces.

Up in the Gods

A peat and slate path beats a tortuous route by the cwm's cliff edge up on to the ridge, and you discover why you came up here in the first place. You find yourself up in the gods, looking over a stage where there's a cast of thousands. At the front, the green cloaked Dee Valley weaves its way though the heather hills of Llangollen and the jagged Aran mountains towards the chorus line, where Cadair Idris, the Rhinogs, and Snowdon parade themselves aloof and often with their heads in the clouds. In the alternative theatre at your back, the Tanat Valley scenery of fields and hedges gives way to the little blue hills of Cheshire and Shropshire in England.

The Berwyns are one of the few places in Wales where the cloudberry grows. These shrubs, not unlike a bramble but lacking thorns, cling closely to the ground. You'll have to be up early to get to the sparse fruits first. They belong to the blackberry family but are orange and taste like raspberries.

Cadair Berwyn

At one time everybody assumed that Moel Sych and Cadair Berwyn were, at 2,713ft (827m), jointly the highest Berwyns – the OS maps that walkers used said so. But everyone who walked the Berwyns looked quizzically across to that little rock peak forming Cadair Berwyn's south summit – it seemed higher. When the OS checked their large scale maps they found that, at 2,723ft (830m), it indeed was the 'tops'.

No Warning

Moel Sych is just a broad flat top, with a cairn for you to pat on your way down to the falls. Amid pretty mixed woodland the peaceful Afon Disgynfa trickles playfully over rocks then, without warning, tumbles off the end of the world. Walkers who have made the ascent look on, amazed, then take the gentler zig-zag route down to the same place. Back in Tan-y-pistyll the café awaits!

walk directions

1 From the more easterly, and the smaller, of the two car parks turn right along the road for about 400yds (366m), then turn sharp left to follow a wide grassy track that climbs north-west to enter the cwm of Nant y Llyn. At an obvious fork keep right on a rising track heading north towards the crags of Cerrig Poethion.

2 The track degenerates into a path that traverses hillsides scattered with gorse. Higher up it crosses two streams before reaching Llyn Lluncaws in the moss and heather cwm. Now the path climbs south of the lake and up a shale and grass spur to the left of Moel Sych's crags. Follow the path along the edge of the crags on the right to reach the col between Moel Sych and Cadair Berwyn. From here climb to the rocky south top of the latter peak. The onward trip to the trig point on Cadair Berwyn's lower north summit is straightforward but offers no advantages as a viewpoint.

3 From the south top retrace your footsteps to the col, but this time instead of tracing the cliff edge you now follow the ridge fence to the

walk information

► DISTANCE	5 miles (8km)
► MINIMUM TIME	3hrs
► ASCENT/GRADIENT	1,870ft (570m) ▲▲▲
► LEVEL OF DIFFICULTY	👣👣👣
► PATHS	Well-defined paths and tracks, 7 stiles
► LANDSCAPE	Mountain and moorland
► SUGGESTED MAPS	OS Explorer 255 Llangollen & Berwyn
► START/FINISH	Grid reference: SJ 076293
► DOG FRIENDLINESS	Sheep usually present: dogs should be on lead
► PARKING	Car park 220yds (201m) before Tan-y-pistyll farm/café, where there's another pay car park
► PUBLIC TOILETS	At Tan-y-pistyll pay car park

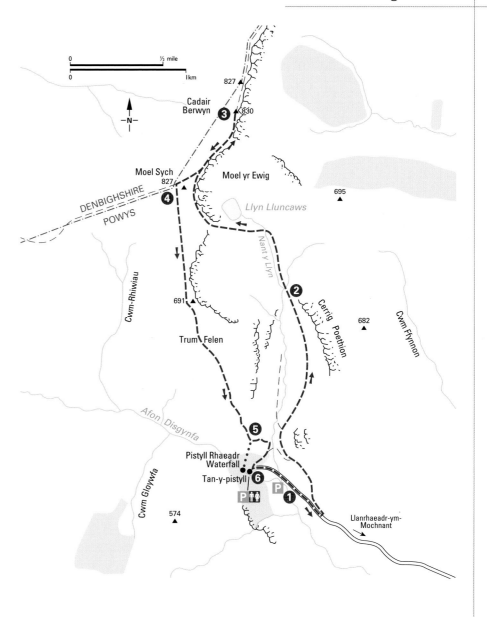

cairn on Moel Sych summit plateau, crossing a stile just before reaching it.

4 Recross the stile and turn right (south) to follow the fence down a wide, peaty spur cloaked with moor grass, mosses and a little heather. Over a slight rise, the path descends again to a stile (wobbly when checked) before dropping into the high moorland cwm of the Disgynfa, where the path is met by a stony track that climbs from the base of the falls.

5 If you want to make a there-and-back detour to the top of the falls, ignore the stony track, and instead go through a gate into the forest and follow the path to the river. If not, descend along the previously mentioned track, which zig-zags down before turning right to head for the Tan-y-pistyll complex. There's a path to the bottom of the falls starting from the café. It leads to a footbridge across the Afon Rhaeadr for the best views.

6 From the café it's a short walk along the road to the car park.

LEFT: A wooded valley at Pistyll Rhaeadr

*One of the finest short walks in Wales, the
Precipice Walk follows a balcony route with
spectacular views of valley, mountain and estuary.*

A Stroll Around the Precipice

ABOVE: *Precipice Walk at Dolgellau*
LEFT: *The Dolgellau countryside is famous
for its unspoiled beauty*

There's been a house at Nannau since the 12th century, when the estate was owned by descendants of Cadwgan, Prince of Powys. That original building was burned down in 1404 after trouble between the owner, Hywel Sele, the 8th Lord of Nannau and his cousin Owain Glyndwr. The pair had never liked or trusted each other, mainly due to Hywel's allegiance to England's House of Lancaster, but they were brought together by the Abbot of Cymer (the abbey in the valley below).

Owain and Hywel

While out hunting together Glyndwr spotted a doe and pointed it out for Hywel to kill. Hywel pretended to aim at the animal but then suddenly swung around towards Owain. The arrow was straight but, as Glyndwr had been wearing armour under his tunic, it did not pierce his skin. After burning down the house it is said that Glyndwr killed his cousin and disposed of his body in a hollow tree. The skeleton wasn't found for 40 years and the house wasn't rebuilt until 1693.

The Nannau family, who became the Nanneys, still lived on the estate. When the male line died out the female line, which had married into the powerful Vaughan family, took over. The Vaughans replanted many of the trees and, in 1796, built the grand mansion that you see today.

Spectacular Views

As you start high there's very little ascent and the early part of the walk eases across woodland and farm pastures. As the path rounds Foel Cynwch and past the Sitka spruce of Coed Dôl-y-clochydd, spectacular views of the wooded Mawddach and Wen valleys open up. The high ridge seen on the other side of the Mawddach is Y Garn, one of the Rhinog outliers. It looks a gentle enough walk from here, but Y Garn's other face is of thick heather and precipitous rock.

Beyond another ladder stile the path itself gets spectacular, taking the form of an exciting terrace, high above the river. Crag, the odd birch and rowan, and flecks of pink from rhododendron bushes all decorate a magnificent scene, which soon adds the great northern cliffs of the Cadair Idris mountains to its repertoire. The precipice lasts an exquisite mile (1.6km) with little twists and turns to add a little spice to the walk. Before long you can trace the Mawddach past Dolgellau's plains, past the sandbars of its estuary, to the sea beyond.

Old Oak Trees

It seems a shame to leave all this behind, but the little path veers left and descends to the shores of Llyn Cynwch where anglers cast for trout. The lake also has an avenue of old oak trees. When you reach the far shores of the lake stop to take one last look south.

RIGHT: *Looking north from Foel Cynwch*

walk directions

1 From the top end of the car park turn right on a level footpath which curves around to join another wide track. The Precipice Walk is a private path around the Nannau Estate, but its use has been authorised by the estate owners since 1890, on the basis that all walkers observe the country code. It's probably one of the finest short routes in Wales and, as such, has been one of Dolgellau's most famous attractions since those early days when Victorian tourists came for their constitutional perambulations. The track swings right at the edge of some fields.

2 Where the track comes to an estate cottage, Gwern-offeiriaid, turn left off it. Follow a clear path leading to the hillside north of Llyn Cynwch. There you see the grand mansion of Nannau, built for the Vaughan family in 1796.

walk information

➤ **DISTANCE**	3 miles (4.8km)
➤ **MINIMUM TIME**	2hrs
➤ **ASCENT/GRADIENT**	Negligible
➤ **LEVEL OF DIFFICULTY**	
➤ **PATHS**	Stony tracks and good paths, occasionally rough, 4 stiles
➤ **LANDSCAPE**	Mountainside and pasture
➤ **SUGGESTED MAPS**	OS Explorer OL18 Harlech, Porthmadog & Bala
➤ **START/FINISH**	Grid reference: SH 745211
➤ **DOG FRIENDLINESS**	Private land – dogs must always be on a lead
➤ **PARKING**	Coed y Groes car park on Dolgellau–Llanfachreth road
➤ **PUBLIC TOILETS**	At car park
➤ **NOTE**	Wear strong footwear as part of route follows narrow path with big drops down to Mawddach Valley. Not a walk for vertigo sufferers

LEFT: The view south along Llyn Cynwch river

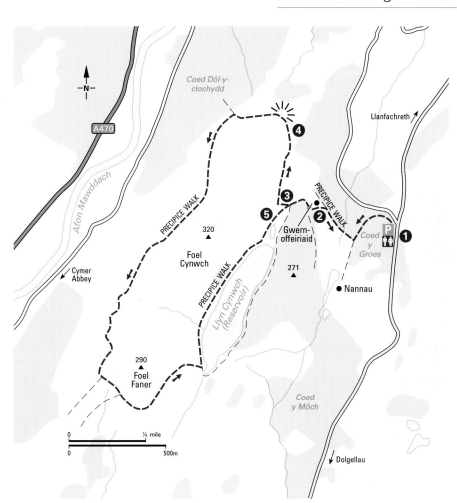

3 At a footpath signpost fork right. The path climbs the hillside and turns northwards by the side of a dry-stone wall.

4 Beyond a stile the footpath curves around a crag-studded hill, with open slopes that give fine views across a green valley below to the village of Llanfachreth and the rugged mountainsides of Rhobell Fawr and Dduallt that lie behind. The footpath edges rounds Foel Cynwch and passes the Sitka spruce woodlands of Coed Dôl-y-clochydd. Ignore a path signed to Glasdir and keep left, reaching the dramatic,

but even ledge path traversing the high hill slopes above the Mawddach Valley. Where the slopes finally ease, there's a promontory on the right, with a bench placed to enjoy the view. The path now arcs round to the southern side of Foel Faner, drops to the lake and turns sharp left to follow the western shore.

5 The path meets the outward route by the hill footpath sign. Retrace the outward route past the estate cottage of Gwern-offeiriaid and through the woods back to the car park.

*See how the Earls of Powis lived as you
walk through their deer park and past
their huge red palace on the hill.*

Powis Castle and the Montgomery Canal

A prosperous and bustling market town set amid rolling green hills, wood and hedgerows, Welshpool has always been synonymous with the River Severn, which flows through it. It was the Severn that brought trade to the town, for it was navigable by boat. The town was, until 1835, known as Pool and some of the old mileposts still refer to Pool. The 'Welsh' was added to distinguish the place from Poole in Dorset.

*ABOVE: The Powys Railway steams through
the Welsh countryside at Welshpool
RIGHT: Powis Castle was home to a dynasty
of Welsh princes*

A Majestic Setting

When you walk up the busy High Street today you'll notice the fine architecture, most of it dating from Georgian times, like the Royal Oak Hotel, but also many older half-timbered buildings. Almost every tourist who comes to Welshpool comes to see the fine castle of Powis. On this route you turn off through the impressive wrought-iron gates before strolling along the long drive through the estate's parklands. Proud oaks are scattered on the well-mown grasslands and a majestic scene is set when you see deer roaming among the trees, maybe antlered stags, or those cute little fallow deer.

Today the castle is a grand red mansion, with castellated ramparts, tall chimneys, rows of fine leaded windows and 17th-century balustraded terraces looking over manicured lawns and neatly clipped yews. Lead statues of a shepherd and shepherdess survive from those early days and keep watch over the colourful shrubs and perennial borders.

Warring Princes

However, the scene would have been so different in 1200, when the castle was first built for the warring Princes of Powys. The battlements would have been there, but there would have been no elegant windows or pretty gardens, for this place was designed to repel enemies, both English and Welsh: more often than not Powis sided with the English, even against the Glyndwr rebellion. The fact that Powis has been continuously occupied has meant that it has made a successful transition from fortress to a comfortable grand mansion.

In 1587 the powerful Herbert family, who became the Earls of Powis, took possession of the castle. They were to reside here until 1988, when the 6th Earl died, and were responsible for the transition. Only for a brief period, when they were attacked by Cromwellian forces and replaced by their bitter rivals, the Myddletons of Chirk, were the Royalist Herberts displaced.

On leaving the castle behind, you are in rural Wales and you descend to the tow path of the Montgomery Canal at the Belan Locks. Built by three different companies and opened in stages from 1796, the canal was designed for narrowboats. Today it is a quiet backwater and a pleasant return route to the wharf at Welshpool.

RIGHT: Colourful flowers at Powis Castle

walk information

➤ **DISTANCE**	4 miles (6.4km)
➤ **MINIMUM TIME**	2hrs
➤ **ASCENT/GRADIENT**	328ft (100m) ▲▲▲
➤ **LEVEL OF DIFFICULTY**	👫👫👫
➤ **PATHS**	Tarmac drive, field path, canal tow path, 3 stiles
➤ **LANDSCAPE**	Country town, parkland and canal
➤ **SUGGESTED MAPS**	OS Explorer 216 Welshpool & Montgomery
➤ **START/FINISH**	Grid reference: SJ 226075
➤ **DOG FRIENDLINESS**	Dogs not allowed on the Powis Castle Estate
➤ **PARKING**	Large pay car park off Church Street in Welshpool
➤ **PUBLIC TOILETS**	By information centre in car park

walk directions

1 From the main car park go past the tourist information centre then go left along Church Street. At the crossroads in the centre of town turn right to head up Broad Street, which later becomes High Street.

2 When you get to a point just beyond the town hall, turn left past a small car parking area and pass through the impressive wrought iron gates of the Powis Castle Estate. Now follow the tarmac drive through the park grounds and past Llyn Du (which means the black lake in English).

3 Take the right fork, the high road, which leads to the north side of the castle. You can detour from the walk here to visit the world-famous gardens and the castle with its fine paintings and furniture and works of Indian art collected by Robert Clive. Continue on the walk on the high road

and follow it past two more pools on the left and the Ladies Pool on the right to reach a country lane.

4 Turn left along the country lane. Opposite the next estate entrance leave the lane over a stile beside a gate on the right, from which a grass track winds down to a bridge. Climb away beside the right-hand fence. Continue over another stile in the corner along an old way, which gently falls to a lane beside the Montgomery Canal. This canal, which runs for 33 miles (53km) from Welsh Frankton in Shropshire to Newtown in Powys, is gradually being restored. You may see a number of narrowboats cruising along this section.

5 Turn over the bridge at Belan Locks, immediately dropping left to the canal tow path. Head north along the canal, later passing beneath the main road. Entering Welshpool, remain on the tow path, passing the Powysland Museum and Montgomery Canal Centre (on the opposite bank), with its exhibits of local agriculture, crafts and the canal and railway systems. Beyond a short aqueduct and former railway bridge, climb out to the road and turn left back to the car park.

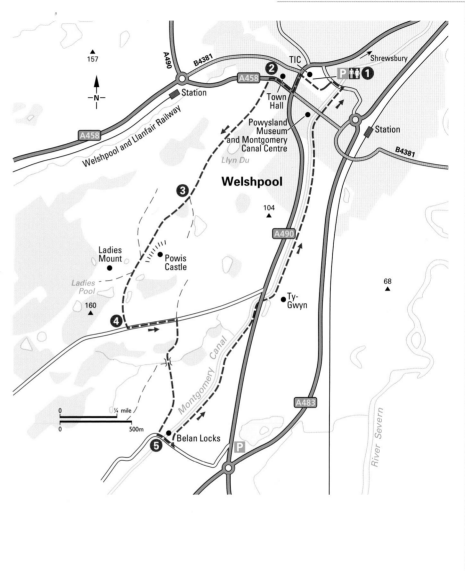

FAR LEFT: Powis Castle atop Ladies Mount near Welshpool
LEFT: The grounds and terraces of Powis Castle

Explore the valleys where the princes of Wales held out against Edward I and a barefoot girl inspired a world-renowned society.

The Dysynni Valley and Castell y Bere

ABOVE: *Castell y Bere near Cadair Idris*
LEFT: *The viewpoint below Foel Fawr at Furnace*

Abergynolwyn lies in the emerald valley of the Dysynni and beneath the great spruce woods of the Dyfi Forest. It's a village built out of Welsh slate and from the proceeds of that slate. However, on this walk we turn our backs on the purple rock to head northwards for the rolling green hills and the delectable oak woods of Coed Cedris that cloak their lower slopes. At the top of these woods you're transported into a high cwm. The Nant yr Eira trickles out from the rushes, but by the time you're descending into the valley of the Cadair, it's splashing and cascading through its own shady ravine.

Mary Jones

Through more woodland, you come to the valley bottom at Llanfihangel-y-pennant, where there's an attractive stone-built chapel that dates back to the 12th century. These days it's dedicated to Mary Jones, a poor weaver's daughter of the 18th century. As a 15-year-old she decided she wanted a Welsh-language Bible of her own. Though she had no shoes to wear, Mary made her way across hills to Bala, some 30 miles (48km) away, where she had heard that some were available. Unfortunately for Mary, the Revd Thomas Charles had none left to sell but, touched by her persistence, he gave her his own copy. Charles was very impressed by Mary's tenacity and it inspired him to consider the needs of Christians around the world who couldn't read the Bible in their own language. Along with several like-minded evangelicals, in 1804 he founded a group called the British and Foreign Bible Society. As well as Bibles in Welsh, one of the first they produced was in Mohawk. Mary's cottage, Tyn-y-ddol, and a monument to her, can be found a short way north up the road.

Welsh Fortress

The main route heads in the opposite direction. Here the Afon Cadair has formed a wide flat valley. In the middle of the plains, perched on a great crag are the ruins of a true Welsh fortress, Castell y Bere. Built in the early 13th century by Llewelyn the Great, it held out longer than any other when Edward I and his armies invaded Wales. By this time Llewelyn ap Grufydd had become Prince of Wales, but had been killed at Builth, leaving his brother Dafydd to defend the castle. Dafydd fought long and hard but was defeated in 1283.

He escaped capture for a while and hid out on the slopes of Cadair Idris. Eventually, he was betrayed by his own people and was dragged to Shrewsbury where he was brutally hung, drawn and quartered. So Wales was defeated and the castle laid waste.

Narrow Defile

The path continues along the now peaceful pastures of this pleasant valley to meet the Dysynni which has wriggled through a narrow defile between two hills. The winding green track that squeezes through with it is perhaps the finest mile in this book; you're almost disappointed to get back to Abergynolwyn so soon.

walk information

➤ **DISTANCE**	5 miles (8km)
➤ **MINIMUM TIME**	3hrs
➤ **ASCENT/GRADIENT**	656ft (200m) ▲▲▲
➤ **LEVEL OF DIFFICULTY**	🐾🐾🐾
➤ **PATHS**	Field paths and tracks, 14 stiles
➤ **LANDSCAPE**	Pastured hills and valleys
➤ **SUGGESTED MAPS**	OS Explorer OL23 Cadair Idris & Llyn Tegid
➤ **START/FINISH**	Grid reference: SH 677069
➤ **DOG FRIENDLINESS**	Dogs should be on leads at all times
➤ **PARKING**	Car park by community centre in Abergynolwyn
➤ **PUBLIC TOILETS**	At community centre

walk directions

1 Cross the road to the Railway Inn and take the lane signposted to Llanegryn. At the far side of the bridge spanning the Dysynni river, turn right through a kissing gate and trace above the north banks. At a second step stile the path turns left before climbing some steps alongside some tall leylandii to reach a country lane.

2 Turn right along the lane which heads east through the Dysynni Valley and beneath the woodlands of Coed Meriafel. At the junction with the B4405 turn left, over a stile and climb north-west across a field. Continue over two more stiles to a woodland path. Follow this to reach a forestry track near the top of the woods.

3 Turn left along the track which climbs out of the woods before veering right to a gate and adjacent stile, giving entry into a large field. Go straight ahead to pick up a ruined

overgrown wall. Where this ends, bear left to descend a high grassy cwm with a stream developing just to your left. Ford another stream which joins from the right near a ruin.

4 The green path develops a flinted surface. Leave it where it starts to climb and rejoin a streamside path on the left. This descends into the woods and stays close to the stream. After passing several cascades it comes out of the woods to reach a track, which in turn leads to the road at Llanfihangel-y-pennant just opposite the chapel.

5 Turn left past the chapel and Castell y Bere (detour through gates on the right for a closer look). Just beyond the castle, take a path on the left that climbs to the gate at the top right-hand corner of the field. Turn right along a green track which passes Caerberllan farm to come to the road. Turn right, go left at the crossroads and cross Pont Ystumanner (a bridge).

6 On the other side, a footpath signpost highlights a track on the left, which passes below Rhiwlas farm and continues as a green path above the river. The path eases across the slopes of Gamallt and swings left with the valley.

7 Beyond a river gorge, the path approaches the back of Abergynolwyn village and turns left to cross an old iron bridge across the river. Turn right along an unsurfaced street to return to the village centre.

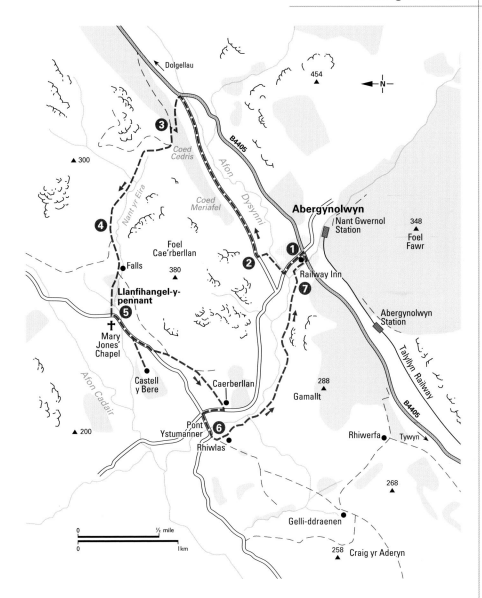

*See Iron Age and medieval castles
and look down on a wide landscape
from Montgomery's Town Hill.*

Montgomery – Land of the Marcher Lords

Montgomery is a fine country town with its origins in medieval times. Tucked beneath a castle-topped crag, many of the houses have Georgian façades, but these were additions to much older dwellings. The centrepieces of the town are the elegant red-brick town hall with a clock tower on top and the half-timbered Dragon Hotel, a 16th-century coaching house. Plaques on the walls of the old houses tell you of Montgomery's proud history, but you can learn more by calling into the Old Bell Inn, which has been converted into a museum.

*ABOVE: Detail of a half-timbered
house in Montgomery
RIGHT: The view across the Severn
Valley from Montgomery Castle*

Controlling the Welsh Marches

After William I conquered England in 1066 he gave the task of controlling the Welsh Marches to his friend and staunch supporter, Roger de Montgomery. Montgomery set up a motte-and-bailey timber castle at Hendomen a mile (1.6km) north of the present town.

Continuous Conflict

There were continuous skirmishes with the Welsh, especially with the coming to power of Llewelyn the Great, Prince of Wales. As a result, Henry III had the current castle built in 1223 on a huge rock overlooking the plains of the River Severn. In 1541 the new English monarch, Henry VII, a Welshman descended from Llewelyn, handed the castle to the Herberts, a powerful Welsh dynasty, who were later to acquire the neighbouring Powis Castle. The castle saw its last action during the Civil War. The Herberts were Royalists and at first held the castle, but in a great battle in which their 5,000 troops were attacked by 3,000 Parliamentarians, it was the Parliamentarians who were finally victorious and in 1649 they demolished the castle. When you view it today though, it's still an impressive place and you get this feeling of impregnability.

The next castle you see on the walk though is much earlier. When emerging from the woods, the sight of the giant earthworks of Ffridd Faldwyn makes it obvious that this hilltop Iron Age fort was of great importance. It was built in four stages, all completed before the Roman conquest. Artefacts, including neolithic tools, are held in the National Museum of Wales in Cardiff.

Distant Views

After making a brief return to the outskirts of Montgomery the route undertakes one of the locals' favourite Sunday strolls – to the top of Town Hill, where the war memorial stands tall. The Automobile Association erected a toposcope to help scan the horizon for the hills of Pumlumon Fawr, Stiperstones, the Clun Hills and the Long Mynd. The Severn can be seen in plan, weaving through forest and field in a landscape as green as any in Ireland.

walk directions

1 From the car park head north, then left along Broad Street, where you'll see the town hall and The Dragon Hotel. A signpost to the castle points up the lane behind, the path then leaving right through a kissing gate. It's a must to see and is free. Return to this point. Head north up Arthur Street, past the Old Bell Museum.

2 Reaching the main road, go left and keep left with the B4385 in the direction of Newtown. Leave just past the speed derestriction sign, over a stile on the left. Bear right across a field towards trees. This path climbs through woodland, then swings left (south-west) to reach the old hilltop fort above Ffridd Faldwyn.

3 Over the stile at the far side of the fort, bear left downfield to the roadside gate. Turn left along the road, which takes you back towards Montgomery.

4 As the road turns sharp right just above the town, leave it for a footpath on the right signposted for the Montgomeryshire War Memorial and beginning beyond a kissing gate. The footpath climbs steadily up the hill to join a farm track, which at first runs parallel to the Town Ditch.

5 As it enters high pastures, the track begins to level out and traverse the eastern hillside. Here you can make a detour to the war memorial that can be seen clearly ahead at the top of the hill. Return to the track and follow it through a gate and past some pens with gorse and hawthorn lining the way on the left.

6 Keep going in the next field, the hedge curving into the corner. Walk ahead through a wide gap and head downfield to leave by a gate and stile at the bottom. Follow a tarmac track down to a junction south-east of Little Mount farm and go left to a lane.

7 Keeping left at successive junctions, walk back to Montgomery. Turn right along Kerry Street into the square.

walk information

➤ **DISTANCE**	5.25 miles (8.4km)
➤ **MINIMUM TIME**	3hrs
➤ **ASCENT/GRADIENT**	951ft (290m) ▲▲▲
➤ **LEVEL OF DIFFICULTY**	🚶🚶🚶
➤ **PATHS**	Well-defined paths, farm tracks and country lanes, 1 stile
➤ **LANDSCAPE**	Pastoral hills overlooking wide plains of the Severn
➤ **SUGGESTED MAPS**	OS Explorer 216 Welshpool & Montgomery
➤ **START/FINISH**	Grid reference: SO 224963
➤ **DOG FRIENDLINESS**	Farming country – dogs should be on lead. Not allowed in castle grounds
➤ **PARKING**	Car park on Bishops Castle Street on B4385 at south end of town
➤ **PUBLIC TOILETS**	Behind town hall

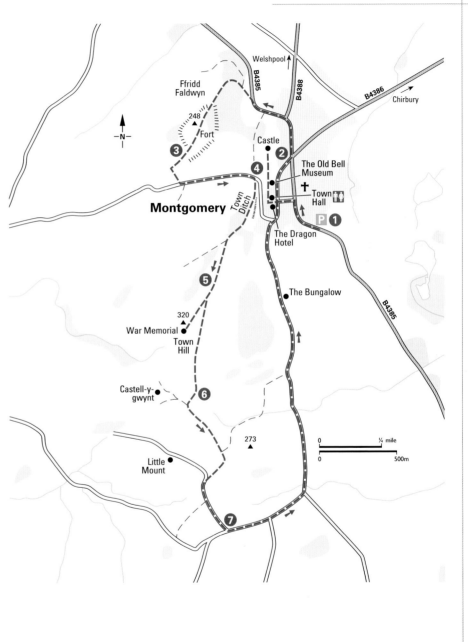

LEFT: *A terrace of colour-washed and brick houses in Montgomery*

*A walk in some of
the wildest countryside
of the Pembrokeshire coast.*

An Invigorating Trundle Around Strumble

This is a favourite stretch of the Pembrokeshire coast, although at times it feels like 'coast path meets the Himalayas', as the narrow ribbon of trail climbs and drops at regular intervals throughout. This is the real wild side of Pembrokeshire.

*ABOVE: Strumble Head lighthouse
RIGHT: A small bridge connects the
islet to the mainland*

High Cliffs

The headland cliffs tower above the pounding Atlantic surf, the path cuts an airy, at times precarious, line across their tops and the sky is alive with the sound of seabirds. Atlantic grey seals, porpoises and even dolphins are regularly spotted in the turbulent waters. Garn Fawr, a formidable rocky tor that lords high above the whole peninsula, brings a touch of hill walking to the experience, and the shapely lighthouse flashes a constant reminder of just how treacherous these spectacular waters can be.

Beacon of Light

Built in 1908 to help protect the ferries that run between Fishguard and Ireland, the Strumble Head Lighthouse guards a hazardous stretch of coast that wrecked at least 60 ships in the 19th century alone. The revolving lights, which flash four times every 15 seconds, were originally controlled by a massive clockwork system that needed rewinding every 12 hours. This was replaced in 1965 by an electrically powered system and the lighthouse was then converted to unstaffed operation in 1980. It's possible to cross the daunting narrow chasm that separates Ynys Meicel (St Michael's Island), where the lighthouse stands, from the mainland by a rickety bridge.

Atlantic Grey Seals

This is one of the best walks in Pembrokeshire to spot these lumbering marine giants that reach over 8ft (2.4m) in length and can weigh as much as 770lbs (350kg). They are usually seen bobbing up and down (bottling) in the water just off the coast, but in autumn when the females give birth to a single pup, they often haul up on to inaccessible beaches where the young are suckled on milk with an incredibly high fat content. The pups shed their white coat after around three weeks, when they are then weaned and taught to swim before being abandoned. The males are usually bigger than the females, with a darker coat and a much more pronounced 'Roman' nose. The best places to see seals on this walk are the bays of Pwll Bach and Pwlluog, near the start.

ABOVE: Strumble Head lighthouse stands on a rocky islet
LEFT: The coast near Carregwastad Point

walk directions

1 Walk back up the road and cross a gate on the left on to the coast path. Pass above the bays of Pwll Bach and Pwlluog, then drop steeply to a footbridge behind the pebble beach of Porthsychan.

2 Follow the coast path waymarkers around Cnwc Degan and down to another bridge, where a couple of footpaths lead away from the coast. Continue along the coast, passing a cottage on the right and climbing and dropping a couple of times, before you reach the obelisk at Carregwastad Point.

3 Follow the main path inland and cross a stile on to a farm track, where you turn right, away from the coast path. Continue with this path, which is vague in places, up through the gorse to a wall, then turn right on to a good track. Take this through a succession of gates and around a left-hand bend.

4 Ignore a track to the right and continue up the cattle track, eventually bearing right into the farmyard where you follow a walkway past livestock pens before swinging left, after the buildings, to the road. Turn right and follow the road past a large house to a waymarked bridleway on the left. Pass Trenewydd and go through a gate on to a green lane. Follow this up to another gate and on to open ground.

5 Turn right here and follow the wall to yet another gate. This leads to a walled track which you follow to the road. Turn left and climb up to the car park beneath Garn Fawr. Turn right, on to a hedged track, and follow this up, through a gap in the wall, and over rocks to the trig point.

6 Climb down and cross the saddle between this tor and the other, slightly lower, one to the south. From here head west towards an even lower outcrop and pass it on the left.

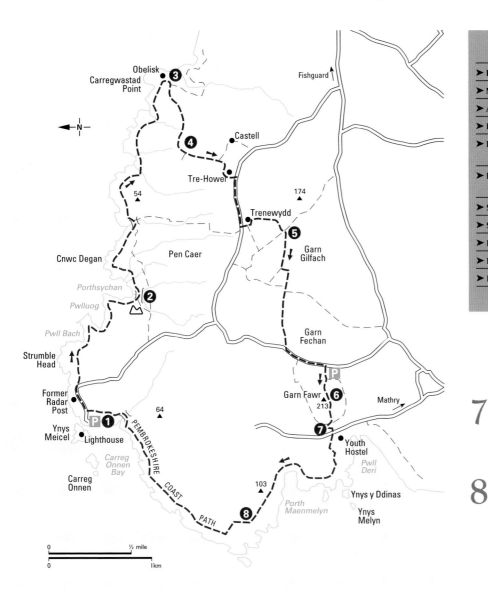

walk information

➤ **DISTANCE**	8 miles (12.9km)
➤ **MINIMUM TIME**	3hrs 30min
➤ **ASCENT/GRADIENT**	920ft (280m) ▲▲▲
➤ **LEVEL OF DIFFICULTY**	👥👥👥
➤ **PATHS**	Coast path, grassy, sometimes muddy tracks, rocky paths, 13 stiles
➤ **LANDSCAPE**	Rugged headland, secluded coves and rocky tor
➤ **SUGGESTED MAPS**	OS Explorer OL35 North Pembrokeshire
➤ **START/FINISH**	Grid reference: SM 894411
➤ **DOG FRIENDLINESS**	Care needed near cliff tops and livestock
➤ **PARKING**	Car park by Strumble Head Lighthouse
➤ **PUBLIC TOILETS**	None en route

This becomes a clear path that leads down to a stile. Cross this and turn left, then right on to a drive that leads to the road.

7 Walk straight across and on to the coast path. Bear right and cross a stile to drop down towards Ynys y Ddinas, the small island ahead. Navigation is easy as you follow the coast path north, over Porth Maenmelyn and up to a cairn.

8 Continue along the coast, towards the lighthouse, until you drop to a footbridge above Carreg Onnen Bay. Cross a stile into a field, then another back on to the coast path and return to the car park.

LEFT: The memorial stone at Carregwastad Point

An easy stroll around the dramatic cliffs of one of mainland Britain's most westerly points.

A Rocky Ramble Around the Head

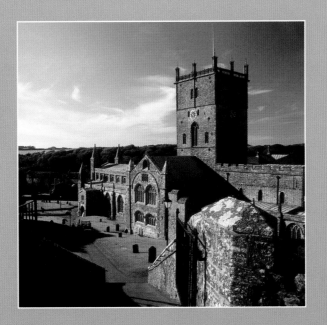

ABOVE: *St David's Cathedral*
LEFT: *The view out to sea from the coastal path at Whitesands Bay*

Steeped in legend, peppered with the evidence of civilisations past, and scenically stunning, it would be difficult to imagine a more atmospheric place than St David's Head. For full effect, visit at sunset and watch the sky turn red over the scattered islets of the Bishops and Clerks.

St David's Head

Carn Llidi, a towering monolith of ancient rock that has all the attributes of a full-blown mountain, yet stands only 594ft (181m) above sea level, dominates the headland. Its heather- and gorse-covered flanks are alive with small heathland birds, which chatter from the swaying ferns and dart for cover in the hidden crannies of dry-stone walls.

The coast, when you meet it, is at its intricate finest; a succession of narrow zawns (clefts), broken up by stubborn headlands that thrust defiantly into the ever-present swells.

The Head itself is magnificent and a few minutes spent exploring will quickly uncover a series of rocky terraces that offer shelter from the wind and stunning views over the ocean to Ramsey Island.

The Warrior's Dyke

Despite its hostile demeanour, St David's Head was once home to a thriving Iron Age community who lived in huts and kept their stock in a field system, the remains of which are still visible. The headland, naturally guarded by the ocean on three sides, was also defended by the Clawydd-y-Milwry (the Warrior's Dyke) at its eastern edge. The dyke is actually formed by three ditches and two ramparts that cut across the neck of the headland. The main bastion, a dry-stone wall that would have once stood around 15ft (4.6m) tall, is still easily visible as a linear pile of stones and rocks. Within the fort there are a number of standing stones, stone circles and the remains of basic huts. The defences are thought to have been built around AD 100.

Burial Chambers

At least 3,000 years older, but well worth seeking out, is Coetan Arthur, a neolithic quoit, or burial chamber, which stands directly above a narrow zawn, bounded on its eastern walls by the red-coloured crags of Craig Coetan, a popular climbing venue. Coetan Arthur consists of a 12ft (3.7m) long capstone, propped up on a smaller rock. The quoit would have originally been covered with earth to form a mound, but this has long since been eroded away. There is evidence of several more burial chambers near the summit of Carn Llidi. Happily both the headland and Carn Llidi are in the care of the National Trust, and you are free to wander at will to investigate these fascinating sites, although you should bear in mind that they are Scheduled Ancient Monuments and protected by law.

walk directions

1 From Whitesands Beach head back up the road, pass the campsite, and a track on the left, and then take the second track on the left. Bear right where it splits and continue around a left-hand bend to walk up to the buildings. Keep left to walk between the houses, then carry on to a gate.

2 Turn right on to the open heathland and follow the footpath along the wall beneath Carn Llidi. Pass the track that drops to the youth hostel on the right and continue around to where the path splits. Take the higher track and keep going in the same direction until, at the corner of a wall, a clear track runs diagonally left towards the coast.

3 Follow this to the coast path, where there's a large fingerpost, and turn left to hug the cliff tops. At Porth Llong, the path bears right to climb to a cairn. The headland is a labyrinth of paths and tracks, but

FAR LEFT: Rock climbers at Porth Clais
LEFT: St Justinian, with Ramsey Island in the backround

75

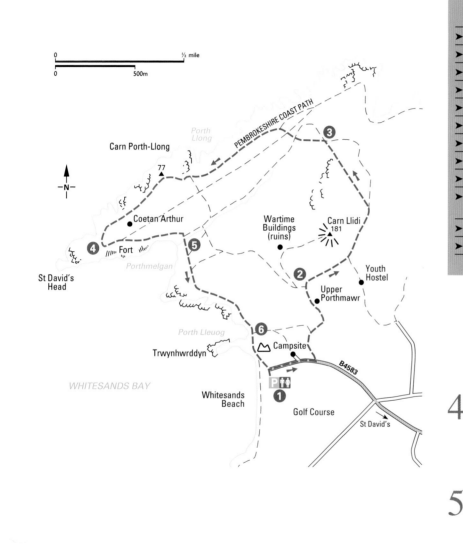

walk information	
➤ DISTANCE	6.5 miles (10.4km)
➤ MINIMUM TIME	3hrs
➤ ASCENT/GRADIENT	850ft (260m) ▲▲▲
➤ LEVEL OF DIFFICULTY	👥👥👥
➤ PATHS	Coast path, 2 stiles
➤ LANDSCAPE	Limestone cliffs and sheltered bays
➤ SUGGESTED MAPS	OS Explorer 164 Gower
➤ START/	Grid reference: SS 467851
➤ FINISH	Grid reference: SS 416881
➤ DOG FRIENDLINESS	Generally fine on bus, care around livestock and on steep cliffs
➤ PARKING	Large car park in Port Eynon
➤ PUBLIC TOILETS	At start and at Rhossili

for maximum enjoyment try to stick as close to the cliff tops as possible as you round a number of narrow zawns. The official coast path doesn't go as far as the tip of the peninsula, but plenty of other tracks do, so follow one as far as you wish.

4 From the tip, turn left and make your way through the rocky outcrops on the southern side of the headland. As you approach Porthmelgan you'll pick up an obvious path that traverses the steep hillside down into a valley, which shelters a small stream.

5 Cross the stream and climb up the steps on the other side. Continue to a kissing gate where the National Trust land ends and maintain your direction. Pass above Porth Lleuog and the distinctive rocky promontory of Trwynhwrddyn, which is worth a visit in its own right.

6 The path then drops steeply down to the road at the entrance to Whitesands Beach.

RIGHT: Walking the Pembrokeshire Coast Path at Whitesands Bay

*A demanding trek along
the ridges of the southern
end of the Vale of Ewyas.*

Llanthony and its Hills

The sheer size of the Vale of Ewyas means that it's best explored in two different walks. This walk tracks south from Capel-y-ffin to loop around the tiny settlement of Llanthony. This circuit has the added advantage of passing the ruins of Llanthony Priory and the opportunity of a great pub at the half-way stage. The down side is that the head of the valley is some way to the north so, in order to follow both ridges, you'll have to drop into the foot of the valley and then climb out again.

ABOVE: *Llanthony Priory*
RIGHT: *Standing among the ruins of Llanthony Priory*

Offa's Dyke Path

From the crest of the Ffawyddog ridge the walk will take you south, over the serrated skyline of Chwarel y Fan, site of disused quarries and, at 2,227ft (679m), the highest point of the day. The ridge then drops steadily down to Bal-Mawr, where you'll follow the banks of the Bwchel brook, through Cwm Bwchel, to the hamlet of Llanthony. From the priory, it's up again, easily at first as you cross the fields adjacent to the ruins, but then steeply to gain a blunt spur that leads on to the slim ridge of Hatterrall. Offa's Dyke Path follows the crest of the ridge, as does the border. Another steep drop brings you back to the pastures above Capel-y-ffin, where you'll pass two tiny, whitewashed chapels before you reach the road.

Ancient Boundary

In an attempt to keep the Welsh to the west, King Offa, the 8th-century ruler of Mercia (Central England), decided to mark out his borders using a deep ditch and an earth wall to strengthen any natural boundaries such as rivers or ridges. It ran from Prestatyn, on the North Wales coast, to Chepstow, at the mouth of the River Wye. In places it was over 20ft (6m) high and 60ft (18m) wide.

walk directions

1 Walk towards the bridge, but before you cross it, bear left up a narrow lane, signposted to The Grange Pony Trekking Centre. Follow this along the side of the stream and past a footpath on the left, marked by a stone archway. Continue to a drive on the left, again leading to the trekking centre, and follow this up to a cluster of barns.

2 Keep right here and continue uphill to a large house on the right, with a gate blocking your progress ahead. Bear around to the left and climb on a loose rocky track that leads up to another gate. Pass through this and follow a rough, eroded track as it zig-zags up on to easier ground. Cross the source of a small stream, and continue to the foot of a steep zig-zag track that climbs steeply up the escarpment.

3 Follow this, bearing both right and left and then, as the gradient eases, continue ahead on a broad and often boggy track. Take this past a few small cairns to a large one, the Blacksmith's Anvil, that sits on top of the ridge. Turn left here and continue to follow the track south over Chwarel y Fan.

4 Walk straight on, along the line of the ridge, to reach the summit of Bal-Mawr. Go down to the left and pass a good track on your left-hand side. Keep ahead to a cairn and then descend to the left. Drop to a fork where you keep right to follow the brook to a crossroads of paths. Maintain your direction (signposted 'Cwm Bwchel').

5 Continue through two fields, down past a house, and over another stile. Ignore another stile on the right and continue down to another at the bottom of the field. Cross this and bear right to cross another and a footbridge. Keep walking straight ahead to another stile and then and continue to a gate. Follow the stream down through another gate to another footbridge. Cross this and take the lane to the road. Turn left here, then turn right to visit the priory.

6 Go through a gate on the left, in front of the priory (signposted to Hatterrall Hill), and follow the main track to a stream, where you turn left to a gate. Continue through a succession of fields and through a small copse to reach an interpretation board. Follow the path up on to the ridge and continue to a crossroads; Offa's Dyke is where you turn left.

7 Walk along Offa's Dyke, pass the trig point and continue for another mile (1.6km) to a cairn and a marker stone at a crossroads of paths. Turn left and follow the path down around a sharp left-right zig-zag to a wall. Turn right here, then turn left over a stile. Walk down, over another stile to a hedge at the bottom of the next field, then turn right to continue to another stile on the left. This leads on to a tarmac lane. Turn right and follow this through a yard, where it becomes a rough track. Keep ahead to a sharp left-hand bend and keep straight ahead, up steps and over a stile. Continue straight ahead through more fields to join another lane and follow this down, past two chapels to the road. Turn left to return to your car.

RIGHT: Llanthony Abbey's ruins are set in lovely countryside

walk information

➤ **DISTANCE**	9.5 miles (15.3km)
➤ **MINIMUM TIME**	5hrs 30min
➤ **ASCENT/GRADIENT**	2,460ft (750m) ▲▲▲
➤ **LEVEL OF DIFFICULTY**	🚶🚶🚶
➤ **PATHS**	Easy-to-follow paths, steep slopes, open moorland, muddy lowland trails, 10 stiles
➤ **LANDSCAPE**	Classic U-shaped valleys topped with broad heather-strewn moorland
➤ **SUGGESTED MAPS**	OS Explorer OL13 Brecon Beacons National Park Eastern area
➤ **START/FINISH**	Grid reference: SO 255314
➤ **DOG FRIENDLINESS**	Some difficult stiles, care needed near livestock. No dogs in grounds of priory
➤ **PARKING**	Narrow pull-in at southern edge of Capel-y-ffin, close to bridge
➤ **PUBLIC TOILETS**	Next to Llanthony Priory

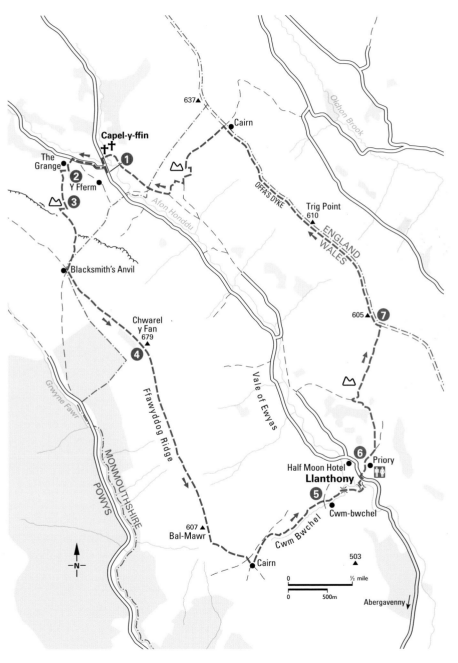

A magical tour of reservoirs, high ridges and the highest mountains in southern Britain.

The Brecon Beacons from the Neuadd Reservoirs

This is a fine way to visit the area's highest ground, as any, or all, of the big peaks can be bypassed if required. It's also an easy way to gain the tops, as it starts at an altitude over 1,300ft (396m) and, with the exception of two short but stiff sections, the climbing remains gentle to the point of being almost undetectable.

ABOVE: *Pen y Fan, the highest point in the Brecon Beacons*
RIGHT: *Pen y Fan, Corn Du and the Tommy Jones Memorial*

Beautiful Valley

The Taf Fechan has certainly carved itself a beautiful valley. Its grand sweeping architecture doesn't appear any the worse for the addition of the two Neuadd reservoirs. The lower reservoir, nearest the start, opened in 1884 to provide water for Merthyr Tydfil, which during the early days of the Industrial Revolution had become something of a boom town. As the iron and steel production increased, and with it the local population, demand started to outstrip supply and the valley was dammed again, this time higher up.

High Peaks

Once up, the walk cruises easily along the sandstone promenade of Graig Fan Ddu and Craig Gwaun Taf, offering great views across the magnificent cwm to the steep head of the valley, where the two highest peaks in southern Britain preside. It also rewards the walker with some tantalising glimpses of the stunning and seldom-visited valley of Cwm Crew, which runs south-west from the narrowest section of the ridge at Rhiw yr Ysgyfarnog – the Slope of the Hare. The high peaks need little introduction. Their might and stature are clear from almost any viewpoint, although you may find yourself surprised by the sheer scale of the drop from the north face of Corn Du and the incomparable north-east face of Pen y Fan, which falls precipitously down more than 1,000ft (305m) to the rolling moorland of Cwm Sere below. Not so surprising are the views from the top which, as you would expect, are magnificent and matched only by the elation of reaching the summit. Incidentally, the correct pronunciation of the peak's name is 'van'; the 'f' is pronounced as a 'v' in Welsh. As you'd expect, the highest peaks also act as a divide for the watersheds, with the water to the north draining into the Usk and the hills to the south feeding the Taff, which runs south to Cardiff.

LEFT: A walker taking the Roman road past the Neuadd Reservoirs

To an Ancient Track

Steep and rocky ground leads down from the table-top summit, with the grassy flanks of Cribyn appearing much steeper than they really are up ahead. If you don't think you can manage another climb, sneak around the peak to the right, otherwise, more fine views await you on the cramped summit. This time you can gaze north over Cwm Cynwyn, as fine a natural amphitheatre as you're ever likely to see. With the peaks bagged, you'll drop into the atmospheric rocky saddle of Bwlch ar y Fan and pick up an ancient track, known locally as the 'Gap Road'. Although many claim it is of Roman origin, the exact age of the track isn't known. It does, however, afford easy progress for tired legs back down to the reservoirs. The grassy shores of the lower lake make a great sun-trap and an excellent picnic spot from where you can look back up the valley to the impressive outlines of the mountains you've just climbed.

walk directions

1 Continue up the lane to a small gate, which leads into the grounds of the reservoir. Bear slightly left on to a narrow path that drops to cross a concrete bridge that spans the outflow. Climb up on to the bank opposite and bear left to walk along its top. This will take you to a gate that leads out on to open moorland.

2 Go through this and keep straight ahead, taking the left-hand of the two tracks, which leads easily uphill towards the edge of a mainly felled forest. Follow the clear track up, with the forest to your left, and then climb steeply up a stony gully to the top of the escarpment.

3 Once there, turn right on to the obvious path and follow the escarpment along for over 2.5 miles (4km). You'll eventually drop into a distinct saddle with the flat-topped summit of Corn Du directly ahead. Where the path forks, keep straight ahead and climb easily up on to the summit. Follow the escarpment edge along and then drop down into another saddle, where you take the path up on to the next peak, Pen y Fan.

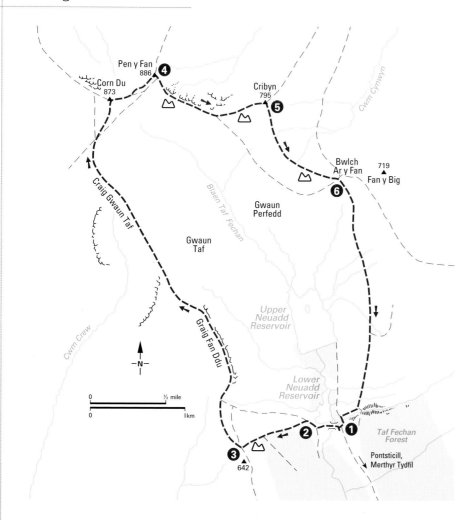

walk information	
➤ **DISTANCE**	7.5 miles (12.1km)
➤ **MINIMUM TIME**	4hrs
➤ **ASCENT/GRADIENT**	2,395ft (730m) ▲▲▲
➤ **LEVEL OF DIFFICULTY**	🅰🅰🅰🅰
➤ **PATHS**	Clear well-trodden paths, boggy patches, broad rocky track, no stiles
➤ **LANDSCAPE**	Steep rocky escarpments overlooking deep U-shaped valley and two small reservoirs
➤ **SUGGESTED MAPS**	OS Explorer OL12 Brecon Beacons National Park Western & Central areas
➤ **START/FINISH**	Grid reference: SO 032179
➤ **DOG FRIENDLINESS**	Care needed near livestock, several steep drops
➤ **PARKING**	At end of small lane leading north from Pontsticill
➤ **PUBLIC TOILETS**	None en route

RIGHT: A viewing platform looks out from Fan y Big over Cribyn, Pen y Fan and Corn Du

4 Again, from the summit cairn, follow the escarpment around and drop steeply, on a rocky path, down into a deep col beneath Cribyn. Keep straight ahead to climb steeply up to the cairn on the narrow summit. Note: this climb can be avoided by forking right and following another clear path that contours right around the southern flanks of the mountain and brings you out at Point 6.

5 From the top, bear slightly right and follow the escarpment around to the southeast. After a long flat stretch, you'll drop steeply down into to a deep col known as Bwlch Ar y Fan.

6 Turn right on to the well-made track that leads easily down the mountain. Go through a gate and follow this for over 1.5 miles (2.4km), until it starts to swing slightly to the left and drops steeply into a rocky ravine. Turn right here on to a track and take it down to a gate. Go through this, turn left and follow the track to its end. Turn right in front of the gate on to another track that leads back to gate at the head of the lane. Go through the gate and follow the lane back to the start.

A low-level walk among riverside scenery with four breathtaking waterfalls.

Along the Waterfalls

In a National Park justly renowned for its sweeping, but barren, mountain scenery, lovers of high ground are in danger of completely overlooking one the Brecon Beacons' hidden gems. This is the pocket of dramatic limestone scenery often referred to as Waterfall Country. South of the upland plateaux of Fforest Fawr, geological faults and water erosion have produced a series of deep, narrow gorges, sheltered by impressive woodland and randomly broken up by a succession of gushing waterfalls.

ABOVE: Inside the Dan yr Ogof caves
RIGHT: Sgwd y Eira waterfall in the Vale of Neath

The highlight of this is Sgwd yr Eira, where it's possible to venture right behind the falls. Walking here is a completely different experience to that of the windswept escarpments, but the scenery is marvellous and the generally sheltered nature of the terrain makes it an ideal outing for those days when cloud obscures the peaks.

Hard Sandstone Shelves

In simple terms, the falls are the result of a geological fault that pushed the hard sandstone, which makes up the backbone of most of the National Park, up against softer shales. The force of the rivers, which spring up high on the mountains of Fforest Fawr, has eroded the shales leaving shelves of the harder rock exposed. These shelves are clearly visible on most of the waterfalls.

Caves and Sinkholes

At the southern edge of the high ground, a layer of carboniferous limestone overlies the old red sandstone. This younger rock is soluble in the slightly acidic rain and river water that constantly pounds it. The erosion results in caves like Porth yr Ogof at the start of this walk, where the rivers literally disappear underground, and craters where rainwater exploits weaknesses and faults in the rock – these are often referred to as sinkholes or shake holes.

LEFT: You can walk behind the Sgwd yr Eira waterfall

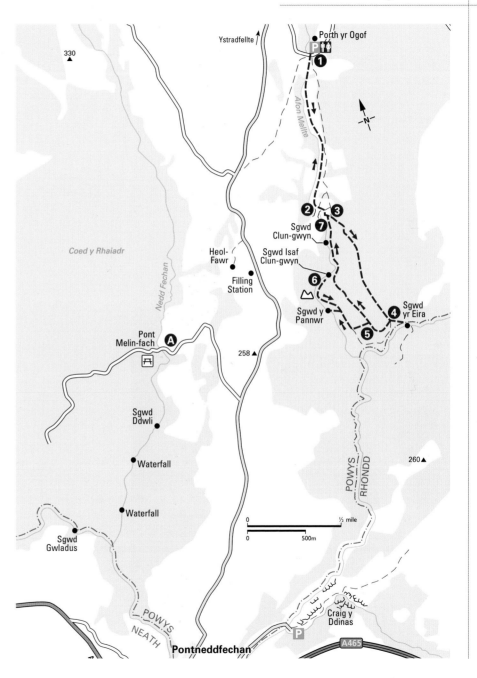

walk information

➤ **DISTANCE**	4 miles (6.4km)
➤ **MINIMUM TIME**	2hrs
➤ **ASCENT/GRADIENT**	360ft (110m) ▲▲▲
➤ **LEVEL OF DIFFICULTY**	🥾🥾🥾
➤ **PATHS**	Riverside paths and forest tracks, some rough and very sections and steps, no stiles
➤ **LANDSCAPE**	Wooded valleys, fast flowing rivers, waterfalls
➤ **SUGGESTED MAPS**	OS Explorer OL12 Brecon Beacons National Park Western & Central areas
➤ **START/FINISH**	Grid reference: SN 928124
➤ **DOG FRIENDLINESS**	Rivers too powerful for fetching sticks and care needed near steep drops
➤ **PARKING**	Park car park at Porth yr Ogof, near Ystradfellte
➤ **PUBLIC TOILETS**	At start

walk directions

1 Cross the road at the entrance to the car park and head down the left-hand of the two paths, waymarked with a yellow arrow. Ignore a right fork marked 'Cavers Only' and follow the main path through a kissing gate and on to the river bank. Now keep the river to your right to follow a rough footpath through a couple more kissing gates to reach a footbridge.

2 Don't cross but continue ahead, to climb steeply up to a fence. Stay with the path, with a wooden fence now on your right, for a few paces and you'll reach a junction of footpaths marked with a large fingerpost. Bear sharp left on to a well-surfaced track, waymarked to Gwaun Hepste, and follow this for a short distance to another junction, where you should turn right (waymarked 'Sgwd yr Eira').

3 Continue on the well waymarked forest trail until another fingerpost directs you right, downhill. Follow this track to the edge of the forest and then bear around to the right. This track leads to the top of a set of wooden steps, on the left.

4 Go down the steps to Sgwd yr Eira (Waterfall of the Snow) and then, having edged along the bank and walked behind the falls (waterproofs recommended), retrace your steps back up to the edge of the wood. Turn left and continue, still following the red-banded posts, to a fork marked with another fingerpost.

5 Turn left here (waymarked to Sgwd Isaf Clun-gwyn Isaf) and descend to the riverside. Turn left again to Sgwd y Pannwr (Fullers Falls), then turn around to walk upstream to Sgwd Clun-gwyn Isaf (Lower Waterfall of the White Meadow). Take care, the ground is very steep and rough around the best viewpoint.

6 Retrace your steps downstream to your original descent path and turn left to climb back up to the fork at the top. Turn left and follow the red-banded waymarkers along to Sgwd Clun-gwyn Isaf, where there's a fenced viewing area. From here, continue along the main trail to the place where you split off earlier.

7 Drop back down to the footbridge and continue along the riverbank to Porth yr Ogof.

LEFT: Sgwd y Pannwr waterfall

An easy walk around a windswept headland overlooking two offshore islands and a marine nature reserve.

Island Views from the Marloes Peninsula

ABOVE: Druidston, St Brides Bay

The Marloes Peninsula forms the westernmost tip of the southern shores of St Brides Bay. The paddle-shaped headland is a popular place to walk due to the narrow neck that affords minimum inland walking for maximum time spent on the coast. It is famous for its stunning scenery, which includes two of the Pembrokeshire Coast National Park's finest and least-crowded beaches, some secluded coves that are often inhabited by seals, and the wonderfully rugged coastline.

Wildlife Sanctuary

Skomer is the largest of the Pembrokeshire islands and is one of the most significant wildlife habitats in the whole country. The island, separated from the mainland by the rushing waters of Jack Sound, measures approximately 1.5 miles (2.4km) from north to south and 2 miles (3.2km) from east to west. It was declared a National Nature Reserve in 1959 and, as well as the protection it receives as part of the National Park, it's also designated as a Site of Special Scientific Interest (SSSI), a Special Protection Area (SPA) and a Geological Conservation Review Site (GCR). Much of the land is a Scheduled Ancient Monument, courtesy of a number of clearly visible Iron Age settlements and enclosures. The sea that surrounds the island is a Marine Nature Reserve, one of only two in the United Kingdom .

Puffins and Shearwaters

The two stars of the Skomer show are the diminutive but colourful puffin and the dowdy and secretive Manx shearwater. Puffins need little introduction; their colourful beaks and clown-like facial markings put them high on everybody's list of favourite birds. There are around 6,000 nesting pairs on Skomer. They arrive in April and lay a single egg in a burrow. The chick hatches at the end of May and the adult birds spend the next two months ferrying back catches of sand eels for their flightless offspring. After around seven weeks of this lavish attention, the chick leaves the nest, usually at night, and makes its way to the sea. Assuming that it learns to look after itself successfully, it will spend the next few years at sea, only returning when it reaches breeding maturity.

walk information

➤ **DISTANCE**	6 miles (9.7km)
➤ **MINIMUM TIME**	2hrs 30min
➤ **ASCENT/GRADIENT**	420ft (128m) ▲▲▲
➤ **LEVEL OF DIFFICULTY**	👣👣👣
➤ **PATHS**	Coast path and clear footpaths, short section on tarmac, 9 stiles
➤ **LANDSCAPE**	Rugged cliff tops and beautiful sandy beaches
➤ **SUGGESTED MAPS**	OS Explorer OL36 South Pembrokeshire
➤ **START/FINISH**	Grid reference: SM 761089
➤ **DOG FRIENDLINESS**	Care near cliff tops and poop scoop on beaches
➤ **PARKING**	National Trust car park above Martin's Haven, near Marloes village
➤ **PUBLIC TOILETS**	Marloes village

Bashful Birds

The mouse-like shearwater is slightly larger than the puffin but it also lays its single egg in a burrow, overlooking the sea. It may not be as obviously endearing as its painted neighbour, especially as most visitors to the island never actually see one, but it's a beautiful and fascinating bird in its own right and there are in fact around 150,000 pairs on Skomer, Skokholm and Middleholm; which amounts to about 60 per cent of the world's total population. The reason they are seldom seen is because they are fairly vulnerable to predators on land so they leave the nest at dawn and spend the whole day at sea, not returning to their burrow until it's almost dark. A careful seawatch at last light may reveal them gathering in huge rafts just offshore or even endless lines of flying birds returning to the island – against the sunset, it's quite a magical sight.

LEFT: The sandy beach seen from Red Cliff
RIGHT: Cliffs border St Brides Bay

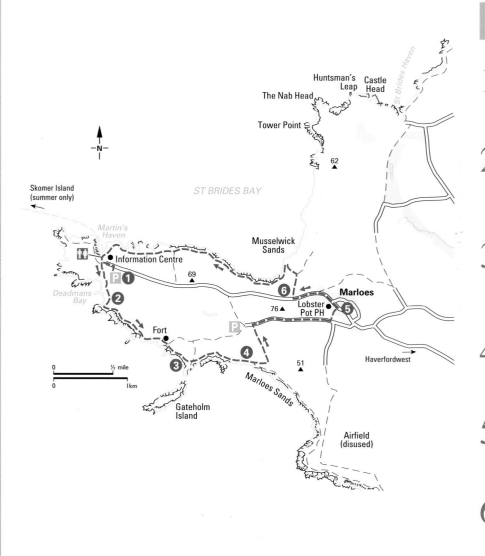

Skomer Island
(summer only)

ST BRIDES BAY

The Nab Head

Huntsman's
Leap

Castle
Head

St Brides Haven

Tower Point

62
▲

Martin's
Haven

Information Centre

Musselwick
Sands

P ❶

69
▲

Deadmans
Bay

❷

❻

Marloes

Fort

P

76 ▲

Lobster
Pot PH

❺

❹

❸

51
▲

Haverfordwest

Marloes Sands

0   ½ mile
0   1km

Gateholm
Island

Airfield
(disused)

1 From the bottom of the car park, walk down to the bottom of the hill. Bear around to the left, then go through the gate straight ahead into the Deer Park. Turn left and follow the path along to a gate and out on to the coast.

2 With the sea to your right, continue easily along over Deadman's Bay to a stile. The next section cruises along easily, passing the earthworks of an Iron Age fort on the left and crossing another stile as you approach Gateholm Island.

3 It is possible to get across to the island at low tide, but care is needed to scramble over the slippery rocks. To continue the walk, follow the coast path, above the western end of the beautiful Marloes Sands until you drop easily to the main beach access path.

4 Turn left and climb up to the road; turn right here. Follow the road along for around 0.75 mile (1.2km) to a hedged bridleway on the left. Follow this down and turn left into Marloes village.

5 Pass the Lobster Pot on the left and continue ahead to leave the village. Ignore a few tracks on the right, as the road bends around to the left, and continue out into open countryside where you'll meet a footpath on the right.

6 Walk down the edge of the field and bear around to the left to drop back down on to the coast path above Musselwick Sands. Turn left and follow the path west for over 1.5 miles (2.4km) to Martin's Haven. Meet the road and climb past the information centre back to the car park.

RIGHT: Marloes Sands, Pembrokeshire National Park

A short stroll across open farmland before taking in some breathtaking coastal scenery.

Magnificent Manorbier and Swanlake Bay

ABOVE: *The ruined walls of Manorbier Castle*
LEFT: *Inside the ruins of the 12th-century Manorbier Castle*

This is a delightful short walk that runs along the heads of some magnificent cliffs and visits a wonderful and remote sandy cove. The outward leg isn't particularly inspirational, but the narrow lane provides convenient access to the highest ground and the section across farmland is open and breezy, with fine views over the coast. Once reached, the narrow belt of white sand that makes up Swanlake Bay provides ample reward for your efforts. Flanked on both sides by impressive sandstone crags and cut off from easy road access by the farmland that you've just traversed, it sees few visitors and provides a stunning setting for a picnic.

walk information

➤ DISTANCE	3 miles (4.8km)
➤ MINIMUM TIME	1hr 30min
➤ ASCENT/GRADIENT	290ft (88m) ▲▲▲
➤ LEVEL OF DIFFICULTY	⋔⋔⋔
➤ PATHS	Coast path, clear paths across farmland, 3 stiles
➤ LANDSCAPE	Sandy coves and dramatic coastline
➤ SUGGESTED MAPS	OS Explorer OL36 South Pembrokeshire
➤ START/FINISH	Grid reference: SS 063976
➤ DOG FRIENDLINESS	Difficult stiles, poop scoop on beaches. Keep on lead and off grass near house on The Dak
➤ PARKING	Pay-and-display car park by beach below castle
➤ PUBLIC TOILETS	At start

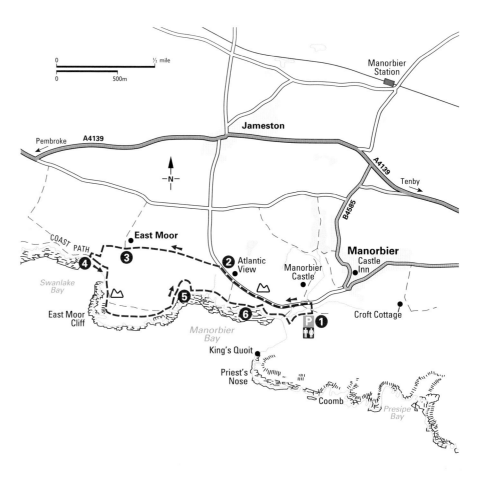

walk directions

1 Walk out of the car park entrance and turn left towards the sea. Stay on the road as it bears around to the right and climbs steeply above the coast. Pass the impressively situated and well-named Atlantic View cottage on your right before reaching a double gate on your left.

2 Cross the stile and walk along the field edge, with a bank and fence on your right, to reach a stone step stile. Cross the stile and continue heading in the same direction to a wooden stile close to the farm which you also cross. Continue to a gate by the farmhouse, which brings you into a small enclosure, then to a wooden stile that leads you away from the buildings.

3 Continue again along the edge of the field to another gate. Go through and turn left to drop down the field edge to a zig-zag that leads on to the coast path. Access to the beach is more or less directly beneath you.

4 Turn left on to the coast path and follow it over another stile and steeply uphill. You'll eventually reach the top on a lovely airy ridge that swings east and then north to drop steeply down into a narrow dip above Manorbier Bay.

5 Cross another stile and climb out of the dip to continue walking easily above the rocky beach. This path leads to a drive, beneath a large house.

6 Continue beneath The Dak and uphill slightly to a gate, where the coast path drops off to the right. Follow this as it skirts a small car park and then winds down through the gorse and bracken to the beach. Cross the stream and turn left to follow a sandy track back to the car park.

ABOVE: King's Quoit, a prehistoric burial chamber in Pembrokeshire National Park

This walk takes in the stunning views over one of Wales's finest and wildest beaches.

The Highs and Lows of Rhossili Bay

Of all the Gower walks this is one of the best, although rather oddly, in its short form, your feet won't leave a single footprint in the sand. The lofty heights of Rhossili Down not only show the magnificent arc of sand in its best light, but they also offer a feeling of spaciousness that's difficult to describe and almost impossible to equal in this part of the world. The ancient stones that define the ridge line only add to the atmosphere.

ABOVE: Rock formations at Mewslade Bay near Rhossili
LEFT: The sun sets beyond the Worm's Head

Area of Outstanding Natural Beauty

The Gower Peninsula comprises a 15-mile (24km) finger of land that points westwards from the urban sprawl of Swansea. Its southern coast is the more spectacular, boasting dune-backed beaches of surf-swept, clean, yellow sand and magnificent limestone cliffs, chiselled in places into deep gullies and knife-edge ridges. The northern coast forms the southern fringes of the marshy Loughor Estuary. It's not as dramatic as the southern coast, but is an important habitat for wading birds and other marine life. Between the two coastlines, the land rises into whaleback ridges, or downs, covered with gorse, heather and bracken and littered with prehistoric stones and remains. Scattered around the windswept landscape are a number of impressive castles. In 1957, the peninsula was designated Britain's first Area of Outstanding Natural Beauty (AONB).

Rhossili Bay and Down

Of all the Gower beaches, none are blessed with quite the untamed splendour of Rhossili Bay. It's sweeping expanse of golden sand runs for more than 4 miles (6.4km) from the headland of the Worms Head to the stranded outcrop of Burry Holms, upon which sits a ruined monastic chapel. It owes much of its wild nature to the steep-sided down that presides over its relentless waves and provides a natural and impenetrable barrier to development. The down is a 633ft (193m) high whaleback ridge that runs almost the full length of the beach. The path that traces the ridge is one the fairest places to walk in the whole of South Wales, especially in late summer when the heather tinges the hillsides pink. From The Beacon, at the southern end of the ridge, the views stretch a long way and it's often possible to see St Govan's Head in Pembrokeshire.

The Worms Head

The string of tiny islets that thrust defiantly into the Atlantic at the bay's southernmost tip are known as the Worms Head. This doesn't refer to the earthworm, but is a derivative of the Old English, Orm, which means dragon or serpent. The likeness can be seen. It is now a nature reserve, but can be reached at low tide by scrambling across the rocky causeway at the western tip of the promontory. It's essential that you check the tide timetables before making such a sortie as it's easy to be cut off by the surprising tenacity of the rising tides.

LEFT: The sandy beach bordering Rhossili Bay

➤ DISTANCE	4 miles (6.4km)
➤ MINIMUM TIME	1hr 45min
➤ ASCENT/GRADIENT	590ft (180m) ▲▲△
➤ LEVEL OF DIFFICULTY	🕴🕴🕴🕴
➤ PATHS	Easy-to-follow footpaths across grassy downs, 2 stiles
➤ LANDSCAPE	Rolling downland, rocky outcrops and views over gorgeous sandy beach
➤ SUGGESTED MAPS	OS Explorer 164 Gower
➤ START/FINISH	Grid reference: SS 416880
➤ DOG FRIENDLINESS	Care needed near livestock
➤ PARKING	Large car park at end of road in Rhossili
➤ PUBLIC TOILETS	At start

walk directions

1 From the car park, head out on to the road and continue uphill as if you were walking back out of the village. You'll pass St Mary's Church on your left then, immediately after this, bear left down on a broad track to a gate at its end. Go through this and keep left to follow a grassy track that snakes along the steep hillside.

2 Follow this through the bracken, passing the Old Rectory on your left and eventually you'll reach a sunken section with a wall on your left, and a caravan park behind. Don't be tempted to break off right just yet; instead, keep going until you come to a gate on the left.

3 Don't go through but turn sharp right and follow the grassy track steeply up on to the ridge. At the top of the steep section it's easy to be drawn off to the right towards some obvious outcrops, but keep to the top track that literally follows the crest.

4 You'll pass some ancient cairns and drop slightly to pass a pair of megalithic cromlechs, or burial chambers. These are known as Sweyne's Howes and are over 4,000 years old. Continue on a broad track up to the high point of The Beacon.

5 Keep straight ahead on a clear track that starts to drop easily then steepens to meet a dry-stone wall. Continue walking down the side of the wall and you'll eventually come to the gate you passed through on the way out.

6 Follow the lane out to the road, turn right and pass St Mary's Church on your right to return to the car park.

LEFT: Sea-sculpted Rhossili Beach
looking towards the Worm's Head
BELOW: Walking near the Worm's Head

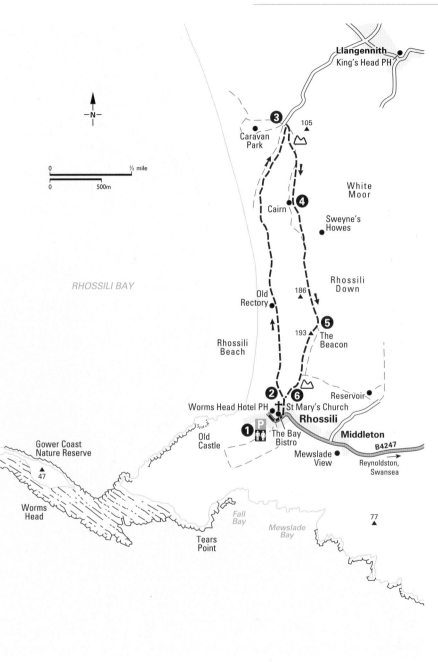

*From a fairy-tale castle to a wild,
windswept hillside – the new-look
Valleys at their scenic best.*

Castell Coch and the New South Wales

A wooded hillside visible from the M4 motorway is hardly the place that you'd expect to find a fairy-tale castle, but at the bottom of the Taff Vale, just a few miles north of Cardiff, is one that will easily rival those of Bavaria. Castell Coch, with its red sandstone walls and conical towers, is worth a visit in its own right, but perched on a cliff top amid stunning deciduous woodland, it's also a great place to start a walk. Conveniently, two waymarked trails run close to the castle and these, together with a labyrinth of forest tracks, provide an invigorating circular route that shows some of the many different faces of the regenerated Valleys.

*ABOVE: The ceiling of the Octagonal Room, Castell Coch
RIGHT: Castell Coch nestles among hills and trees*

Castell Coch

Every bit as captivating up close as it is from a distance, this majestic building, now managed by CADW (Welsh Historic Monuments), was built in the late 1870s on the site of a 13th-century fortress. Unbelievably, it had no military purpose whatsoever but was, in fact, a country retreat for the 3rd Marquess of Bute, who at the time was thought to be the richest man in the world and based his empire in Cardiff.

Fantasy Style

Its design, by the architect William Burges, who also designed St Finbar's Cathedral in Cork, is pure, unadulterated fantasy, with a working drawbridge and portcullis, three circular towers and a dream boudoir that features a lavishly decorated domed ceiling. The grandest of all the castle's rooms has to be the drawing room, three storeys high with a ribbed and vaulted ceiling, further decorated with birds and butterflies. The two-storey chimney piece boasts statues of the Three Fates, which show the thread of life being spun, measured and finally cut. Characters from Aesop's fables are also depicted.

The route away from the woods follows a section of the Taff Trail, a 55-mile (89km) waymarked route that leads from Cardiff Bay to Brecon via the Taff Valley, Llandaff, Pontypridd and Merthyr Tydfil. Most of the trail, including the lower section of this walk, is along disused railway lines, along with forest tracks and canal paths.

From the Taff Trail, this walk follows an airy section of the 21-mile (34km) Ridgeway Walk (Ffordd-y-Bryniau). This trail traces a fascinating hill-top line across what was once the Borough of Taff Ely until the local government reorganisations of the mid-1990s. The section followed climbs steeply on to the narrow ridge of Craig yr Allt, a spectacular viewpoint which on the one hand feels as wild as the mountains further north, but at the same time gives a raven's-eye view of the industrial side of the valleys.

RIGHT: Castell Coch's Kitchen Tower

walk directions

1 From the car park, walk up to the castle entrance and turn to the right to walk to a stone information plaque. Take the path next to this and climb steeply on a good path past a waymark post and through a gap in a fence to a junction of tracks.

2 Turn sharp left, signposted 'The Taff Trail', by a picture of a viaduct, and follow this broad forest track around the hillside and then down, where it meets the disused railway line close to some houses. Pass through the barrier on the right and follow the clear track for over a mile (1.6km) until you pass a picnic area and come to another barrier.

3 Go through the barrier then, as you come to a disused bridge, turn right over a stile, signposted 'Ridgeway Walk'. Take this and follow it up for a few paces and then around to the right. Ignore one turn left and then turn sharp left to zig-zag back across the hillside, where you turn right again. Follow this around to the left again, aiming at the mast and then, as you reach the field edge, bear right once more. This leads up to a post on a narrow ridge where you turn left.

4 Climb steeply up the ridge and continue, with high ground to your left, until you reach a clear path that leads left, up to the ridge top. Follow this and bear right at the top to cruise easily along, with great views. Keep ahead to drop slightly and then bear left on to a broad track.

5 Follow it down through the bracken to a stile. Cross this and take the track down to a gate that leads on to a tarmac drive. Turn left and continue past some houses on the right-hand side to a junction. Turn right and climb up to another junction, where you bear right.

6 Carry on past the golf club, then fork right on to a narrow lane that drops and bears around to the left. Turn right here to walk past the Forestry Commission sign and then turn immediately left, on to a clear footpath marked by a post.

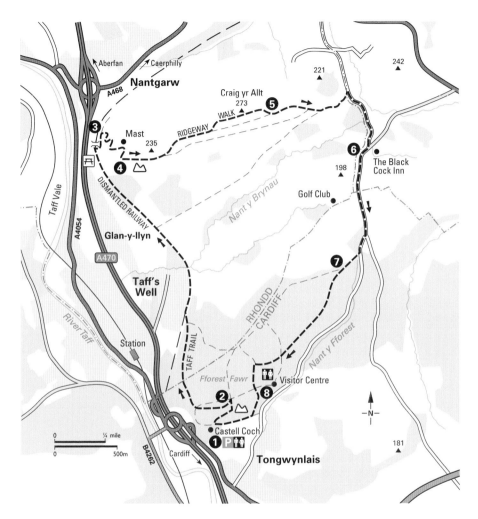

walk information

➤ **DISTANCE**	5.5 miles (8.8km)
➤ **MINIMUM TIME**	2hrs 30min
➤ **ASCENT/GRADIENT**	920ft (280m) ▲▲▲
➤ **LEVEL OF DIFFICULTY**	🚶🚶
➤ **PATHS**	Forest tracks, disused railway line and clear paths, short section of tarmac, 2 stiles
➤ **LANDSCAPE**	Mixed woodland and open hillside with views over residential and industrial developments
➤ **SUGGESTED MAPS**	OS Explorer 151 Cardiff & Bridgend
➤ **START/FINISH**	Grid reference: ST 131826
➤ **DOG FRIENDLINESS**	Care needed near livestock; not allowed in castle
➤ **PARKING**	Castell Coch
➤ **PUBLIC TOILETS**	In castle and nearby Countryside Visitor Centre

7 Follow this path, ignoring tracks on both the right and left, until the posts become blue and you come to a T-junction by a sign forbidding horse-riding. Cross the small brook and turn left to continue steeply downhill, past a turning on the left to the Countryside Visitor Centre.

8 The track eventually swings around to the right and descends to meet the drive. Turn right to climb up the drive and back to the castle.

Walking in Safety

All these walks are suitable for any reasonably fit person, but less experienced walkers should try the easier walks first. Route finding is usually straightforward, but you will find that an Ordnance Survey map is a useful addition to the route maps and descriptions.

Risks

Although each walk here has been researched with a view to minimising the risks to the walkers who follow its route, no walk in the countryside can be considered to be completely free from risk. Walking in the outdoors will always require a degree of common sense and judgement to ensure that it is as safe as possible.

- Be particularly careful on cliff paths and in upland terrain, where the consequences of a slip can be very serious.
- Remember to check tidal conditions before walking on the seashore.
- Some sections of route are by, or cross, busy roads. Take care and remember traffic is a danger even on minor country lanes.
- Be careful around farmyard machinery and livestock, especially if you have children with you.
- Be aware of the consequences of changes in the weather and check the forecast before you set out. Carry spare clothing and a torch if you are walking in the winter months. Remember the weather can change very quickly at any time of the year, and in moorland and heathland areas, mist and fog can make route finding much harder. Don't set out in these conditions unless you are confident of your navigation skills in poor visibility. In summer remember to take account of the heat and sun; wear a hat and carry spare water.
- On walks away from centres of population you should carry a whistle and survival bag. If you do have an accident requiring the emergency services, make a note of your position as accurately as possible and dial 999.

Acknowledgements

The Automobile Association would like to thank the following photographers, companies and picture libraries for their assistance in the preparation of this book.

Abbreviations for the picture credits are as follows: (t) top; (b) bottom; (l) left; (r) right; (AA) AA World Travel Library.

2/3 AA/S Watkins; 5 AA/C & A Molyneux; 6 AA/D Croucher; 7bl AA/C Molyneux; 7bcl AA/C Nicholls; 7bcr AA/N Jenkins; 7br AA/I Burgum; 10/11 AA/H Williams; 12/13 AA/N Jenkins; 13 AA/R Newton; 14/15 AA/S Lewis; 16 AA/N Jenkins; 18 John Hale/Alamy; 18/19 A Room With Views/Alamy; 22/23 AA/S Watkins; 23 AA/C Jones; 24/25 AA/N Jenkins; 26 AA/R Eames; 28 AA/N Jenkins; 28/29 AA/N Jenkins; 32/33 AA/N Jenkins; 33 AA/P Aithie; 34/35 AA/P Aithie; 36 AA/N Jenkins; 38/39 AA/R Eames; 39 AA/N Jenkins; 41 AA/N Jenkins; 42/43 AA/D Croucher; 43 AA/D Croucher; 44 AA/D Croucher; 46/47 AA/D Croucher; 47 AA/D Croucher; 48/49 AA/D Croucher; 50 AA/D Croucher; 52 AA/R Newton; 52/53 AA/N Jenkins; 54/55 AA/N Jenkins; 56 AA; 57 AA/R Newton; 58/59 AA/D Croucher; 59 The Photolibrary Wales/Alamy; 62 AA/R Eames; 62/63 AA/N Jenkins; 65 AA/R Newton; 66 AA/N Jenkins; 66/67 AA/I Burgum; 68 AA/N Jenkins; 69 AA/N Jenkins; 70 AA/N Jenkins; 72/73 AA/I Burgum; 73 AA/N Jenkins; 74 AA/C Warren; 74/75 AA/C Warren; 77 AA/I Burgum; 78 AA/N Jenkins; 78/79 AA/N Jenkins; 81 AA/N Jenkins; 82 AA/I Burgum; 82/83 AA/N Jenkins; 84 AA/C & A Molyneux; 87 AA/N Jenkins; 88 AA/C & A Molyneux; 88/89 AA/I Burgum; 90 AA/I Burgum; 92 AA/I Burgum; 93 AA/C Warren; 94 AA/C Molyneux; 95 AA/R Ireland; 97 AA/C Molyneux; 98/99 AA/S Bates; 99 AA; 101 AA/S Bates; 102/103 AA; 103 AA/I Burgum; 104/105 AA/C Molyneux; 106 AA/N Jenkins; 107 AA/M Moody; 108 AA/I Burgum; 108/109 AA/H Williams; 111 AA/I Burgum

Every effort has been made to trace the copyright holders, and we apologise in advance for any accidental errors. We would be happy to apply the corrections in the following edition of this publication.